A Century of Baseball Lore

A Century of Baseball Lore

John Thorn

Illustrated by Jesse Jacobs

Galahad Books • New York City

Published in 1980 by
Galahad Books
95 Madison Avenue
New York, New York 10016
By arrangement with Hart Publishing Company, Inc.

Library of Congress Catalog Card Number: 80-65144
ISBN: 0-88365-446-6
Printed in the United States of America

Contents

A Century of Baseball Lore

The Early Years

1869-1900

All evidence to the contrary, most fans still believe the official myth of baseball: that the game was invented in Cooperstown, New York in 1839 by a 20-year-old lad named Abner Doubleday. In fact, "basteball" was being played by little English and American boys long before the birth of Doubleday—indeed, long before the birth of Cooperstown itself.

Yet in 1869, when Harry Wright formed the Cincinnati Red Stockings into baseball's first professional team, American baseball, the offspring of cricket, had become the national pastime.

The years 1869-1901 marked the frontier of professional baseball. Like the American frontier itself, baseball was colorful and exciting, rough and sometimes seamy. Umpire-baiting was vicious to a degree undreamed of today, gambling scandals were numerous, and liquor provoked many a brawl on the field.

In this period, rulesmakers were constantly experimenting with innovations that might better balance the primal battle between pitcher and batter. Like the major-leaguers of today, the ball-players of those days played for pay—small pay, indeed, by today's standards. But those stalwarts loved baseball with a fierceness which proved that the game was more to them than just money—and that love for the game they bequeathed to the generations who followed.

It Started in Cincinnati

The history of professional baseball really begins with the Cincinnati Red Stockings. Although individual "amateurs" had been paid under the table for several years, the Reds were the first team to be openly recompensed for their services.

In 1869, the newly formed Red Stockings toured the East and Midwest, playing 66 games without defeat and outscoring the opposition 2,395 to 575. The only blemish on their record was a 17-17 tie played against the Troy Haymakers, who walked off the field in the sixth inning so that gamblers who had laid their money on the Troy nine could avoid paying off. The Reds' winning streak continued into 1870, until the Brooklyn Atlantics snapped the Cincinnati string at 92.

Though the Reds performed beautifully on the field, they were hardly a sensation at the box office. For the year 1869, the team made a net profit of $1.39.

THE STAR OF THE Cincinnati Red Stockings of 1869 was short-stop George Wright. Receiving $1,400, he was the team's highest-

salaried player, and his heroics attest that he was worth every penny of it.

In the 66 games that the Reds played on their 12,000-mile tour, Wright batted .518, scored 339 runs, and belted 59 home runs.

Baseball's First Great Pitcher

In 1870, Rockford defeated the mighty Cincinnati Red Stockings, managed by Harry Wright. The winning hurler was a 20-year-old youth by the name of Albert Goodwill Spalding.

When Wright left Cincinnati the next year to organize a new team in Boston, he invited Spalding to join him. And it was in Beantown that Spalding had his greatest years. After winning 21 games in 1871, over the next four years he went on to post records of 36-8, 41-15, 52-18, and 56-5!

In 1876, Spalding was not quite 26 years old, yet he was signed to manage the Chicago White Stockings. Spalding led his team to the pennant, winning 46 games himself.

Three years later, Spalding retired from active play, and went on to make a fortune in the sporting-goods firm which still bears his name today.

How Fleeting Is Fame!

One of the strangest careers in the history of professional baseball is that of Joseph E. Borden. In 1875, he pitched for the

Philadelphia Athletics under the psuedonym of Joseph E. Josephs. Although his record that year was a mere two wins against four losses, one of his victories was a no-hitter, the very first on record.

The next year was marked by the formation of the National League. On April 22, 1876, the first game in National League history was played in Philadelphia, with the Boston Red Stockings nipping the Athletics, 6-5. The winning pitcher? Joe Borden, by now pitching in Beantown under his own name.

A month and a day later, Borden threw another no-hitter, this one the first in National League history.

But with all these firsts, Borden managed to compile a won-lost record of only 12-12 in 1876. Before the season was over, he was given his walking papers by the brass, and finished the year as the groundskeeper of the Boston ballpark. Joe Borden was then only 22, but he never pitched another big-league game.

ON SEPTEMBER 27, 1881, the Chicago White Stockings were in Troy, New York—then a National League franchise—to play the final game of the season. The Sox had long since clinched the pennant, Troy was locked in fifth place, and the rain was coming down in deluvian fashion. Yet for some mysterious reason, these three incentives not to play the game failed to deter the participants, and Chicago and Troy sloshed on to a conclusion.

What is even more mysterious is that anyone paid good money to see this game. But twelve hardy idiots did, and thus put themselves into the record books as the smallest paid crowd to witness any major-league ballgame.

LIKE A COMET, Tommy Bond shone briefly but ever so brightly. Between 1877 and 1879, he won 40, 40, and 42 games for the Boston Red Stockings. The next season, he slipped to a record of 26-29; and in the last three years of his career, he won a total of only 12 games.

New York's Tim Keefe shone both brightly and durably, and his plaque can be found in the Hall of Fame. Over a seven-year span between 1883 and 1889, Smiling Tim never won less than 30 games, and twice he won over 40. Between June 23 and August 10 of 1888, Keefe won 19 consecutive games without a loss—a record not equaled until Rube Marquard came along in 1912.

A Rough Initiation

In 1883, his first year in the majors, John Coleman won more than three quarters of all the games won by the Philadelphia Phillies. Yet he was hardly a candidate for Rookie-of-the-Year honors—Philly won only 17 games all year. Of these, Coleman won 13, but he also dropped 48 games, more than any other pitcher has ever lost in a single season.

IN SEPTEMBER 1883, Hugh Daly climaxed a season of 24 victories by hurling a no-hitter for Cleveland.

The next year, now wearing the uniform of the Chicago White Stockings, he won 22 games, struck out 19 men in one game, and played second, short, and the outfield when he wasn't pitching.

Not bad for a man with only one arm.

Immortality of a Sort

Larry Corcoran was the premier pitcher of the Chicago White Stockings. Indeed, he was so great an athlete that on the days when he did not go to the box, he sometimes played shortstop. It was on one of these days, in 1884, that Corcoran earned a dubious place in the record books by making the astronomical total of 10 errors.

This experience seems to have left the Chicago ace so shaken that after 1884, he was never again an effective hurler. Between 1880 and 1884, Corcoran won 167 games—an average of nearly 36 wins per season. And he spun three no-hitters. During all of the next three years, he won only six games.

The Workhorse

Frank Bancroft, manager of the Providence team of the National League, was in a real jam. The 1884 season was already in full swing when one of his two star pitchers, Charlie Sweeney, jumped to the Union Association, a rival league. In less than half a season, Sweeney had already won 17 games for Providence. Just a few days earlier, he had struck out 19 batters in one game!

Bancroft was left with only one capable hurler, Charles "Hoss" Radbourn. A 30-year-old righthander, on the days when he did not pitch Hoss played first, second, short, third, or in the outfield. Now that Sweeney was gone, Hoss would have to go to the mound nearly every day.

And go every day he did! Old Hoss pitched every one of the last 38 games on the Providence schedule, and he won the last 18 in a row. Over the full season, Radbourn turned in a fantastic 60 wins while losing only 12. He pitched the herculean total of 673 innings!

In October of that year, Providence met the original New York Mets, champs of the American Association, in a best three-out-of-five World Series. Radbourn pitched the first three games—played on consecutive days—and won all three of them. In this trio, he yielded a total of 10 hits, and didn't allow a single base on balls.

Thus, as a matter of record, Old Hoss completed the greatest year any pitcher has ever had. Though never again did he win even half as many games in any one season, he finished his career with 306 victories and earned himself a well-deserved place in baseball's Hall of Fame.

WHEN BABE RUTH hit 60 homers in 1927, he surpassed the old mark of 59 set by—Babe Ruth, in 1921. And the mark of 59 topped the previous record of 54, collected by the Bambino in 1920. And the 54 shattered the previous pinnacle of 29, attained by the budding Sultan of Swat in the days when he still pitched enough for the Red Sox to garner eight wins.

But the Babe did not always have a monopoly on the home run. In fact, when he walloped 29 in 1919, he bested a mark that had stood for *35 years*—actually longer than Ruth's record of 60 held up. In 1884, Ned Williamson of the Chicago White Stockings, the greatest slugger of the pre-Ruthian era, hit 27 balls for the full distance.

White Sox and Black Players

Adrian "Cap" Anson of the Chicago Nationals was one of the game's greatest players, managers, and innovators. He played for 27 years—longer than anyone else; he hit over .300 on 21 occasions; he amassed over 3,000 lifetime hits; and he fielded brilliantly.

As a playing manager, he led the White Stockings to five pennants in seven years. (When he left Chicago at last, "Pop" Anson's White Stockings became known as the "Orphans.") And Anson is credited with the invention of spring training in 1886, when he took his men to Hot Springs, Arkansas, to boil out the winter's boozing.

But Anson must also take credit for being the single most important force behind the exclusion of blacks from the big leagues.

Contrary to popular assumption, Jackie Robinson was not the first of his race to play in the major leagues. Three black men played in the big time in the 1880's, the first of them being catcher Moses Fleetwood Walker. (The other two were Moses' brother Welday and George H. Higgins.)

In the spring of 1884, when Walker was catching for the minor-league team in Newark, N.J., Anson's Chicagoans came to town to play an exhibition game against them. When he saw that Walker, George Stovey, and another black were in the lineup, Anson pulled his team off the field and refused to play unless the Negroes were removed from the field.

It has been written that Anson went so far as to introduce a resolution, at a meeting of major-league managers and executives, to bar blacks from the game. Whether this is true or not, Anson was certainly an outspoken opponent of black participation in the American Game, and he was undeniably of sufficient stature to sway others to his view.

UNTIL 1872, the only way a pitcher could deliver the ball up to home plate was with an underhand, stiff-armed motion. But in that year, a moundsman was at last allowed to snap his wrist and thus put some zip in his pitch.

By 1884, all restrictions on pitching style were lifted, and professional baseball saw its first overhand pitch. Hurlers enjoyed a banner year, Hoss Radbourn leading the way with 60 wins. This upset the hitters' lobby so much that in 1885 the rules committee was persuaded to allow the use of flat-sided bats, an innovation which lasted eight years.

Kill the Umpire!

Life was never tougher for umpires than it was in the 1880's and 1890's. "Kill the umpire" was no idle threat. Several minor-league umps, in fact, lost their lives on the diamond, and numerous major-league arbiters were assaulted by mobs. The umpire, of course, was a quite common target for pop bottles.

In the popular image of the day, the man in blue merited every bit of abuse that could be heaped upon him. Witness this little ditty, published in 1886:

> *Mother, may I slug the umpire,*
> *   May I slug him right away?*
> *So he cannot be here, mother,*
> *   When the clubs begin to play?*
>
> *Let me clasp his throat, dear mother,*
> *   In a dear, delightful grip*
> *With one hand, and with the other*
> *   Bat him several in the lip.*
>
> *Let me climb his frame, dear mother,*
> *   While the happy people shout;*
> *I'll not kill him, dearest mother,*
> *   I will only knock him out.*
>
> *Let me mop the ground up, mother,*
> *   With his person, dearest, do;*
> *If the ground can stand it, mother,*
> *   I don't see why you can't too.*

Kilroy Was Here

In 1973, Nolan Ryan set a new major-league record for strikeouts in a single season by fanning 383 batters, surpassing the previous modern-era mark of Sandy Koufax by one K.

But when it comes to K's, no one could hold a candle to one Matches Kilroy. As a rookie pitcher with the Baltimore Orioles in 1886, the lefthanded Kilroy threw his smoke past 505 batters.

Mr. Kilroy, it should be related, enjoyed certain advantages denied to Messrs. Koufax and Ryan. In 1886, the pitcher stood only 50 feet from home plate, as contrasted with the modern distance of 60′6″. Moreover, it took seven errant pitches to earn the batter a base on balls.

THE MOST DARING baserunner of all time? Modern players have to take a back seat to Curt Welch. In the tenth inning of the final game of the 1886 World Series, the St. Louis Browns' center-fielder stole home to win the whole shebang. The owner of the Browns, utterly delirious, turned over the total proceeds of the gate, some $15,000, to the players. Forever after, Welch's run for the money was known as "the $15,000 slide."

Four Strikes 'n' You're Out

Who recorded the highest batting average in a single season— Rogers Hornsby, Hugh Duffy, or Tip O'Neill?

No matter whom you chose, you were right.

Rogers Hornsby laid claim to the modern major-league record by hitting .424 for the St. Louis Cardinals in 1924.

Hugh Duffy hit .438 for the Boston Beaneaters in 1894, and is considered to possess the highest batting average in major-league history.

Then what's left for Tip O'Neill? A batting average of .492, and a footnote in the record books. The star outfielder of the St.

Louis Browns had his great season in 1887, the only year when bases on balls were counted as hits, and a batter was allowed four strikes.

In that peculiar year, 12 batters hit over .400. When their averages are recomputed without counting walks as hits, only two are left above the .400 mark, O'Neill being one of these. He would have hit .435. On the other hand, Harry Stovey when his average is recomputed drops from .402 to .286.

O'Neill had as good a year with the stick as anyone has ever had. Besides leading the American Association in batting average, he topped the circuit in runs, doubles, triples, and homers. He undoubtedly would have won the RBI crown, too, but no records were kept of this statistic until 1907.

THE GIANTS of 1930 batted .319 for the season. This fantastic figure is a modern major-league record. But in the early days, Detroit batsmen terrorized National League pitchers with a mark of .347 for the 1887 season.

Dummy Teaches Umps

William Ellsworth Hoy came to the big leagues as a 27-year-old rookie in 1888. He was immediately tagged with the nickname "Dummy"—not because of any deficiencies of intellect, but because he was a deaf mute.

Despite his handicap, Hoy became one of the top players of his day. He played 14 years in the majors, batted .291, and stole 514 bases.

He is also credited with inducing home-plate umpires to raise the right arm to signal a strike, since Hoy couldn't hear the call. Soon umpires began to signal strikes for all batters, thus relieving the strain on their vocal cords and making it easier for the fans to follow the action.

IN 1888 AND 1889, Billy Shindle was the regular third-baseman of the Baltimore Orioles. While not a spectacular performer at the hot corner, he was reasonably steady.

In 1890, following a dispute over an owners' ceiling on salaries, four out of five major-league regulars jumped to the newly formed Players' League. Shindle joined the Players' Philadelphia club where he was installed at shortstop. There, he proceeded to make 115 errors in the 132 games he played.

Billy Shindle went on to play major-league ball for eight years more—but at third base. He was never again trusted to play shortstop, not even for a single inning.

Slide, Kelly, Slide!

Mike "King" Kelly was so brilliant a player in the 1880's that Boston had to pay $10,000, an astronomical sum in those days, to pry him away from the Chicago club. Kelly's innovation of the "hook" or "fadeaway" slide inspired a popular song of the day, "Slide, Kelly, Slide."

As a manager, Kelly was no less brilliant and daring. Sitting on the Boston bench one day, he looked up to see a foul ball coming directly at him. The Boston catcher was racing for the ball, but clearly had no chance of making the grab.

At this time, the rules stated that substitutions could be made at any point in the game. Kelly stood up, announced "Kelly now catching for Boston," and caught the ball. This adroit maneuver stumped the umpire, and led to a rule change the next season: a substitution could be made only when the ball was dead. That rule is still on the books—as Casey Stengel would say, you could look it up.

BUCK EWING, star catcher of the New York Giants in the 1880's and 1890's, was famed for his fleetness of foot. In his most famous exploit, he stole second on one pitch and third on the very next, and then announced to the fans that he was about to steal home.

And he did that, too, with a dashing slide that was reproduced in a lithograph entitled "Ewing's Famous Slide," and was sold all over New York.

All Is Fair...

In the early days, the spitter, the emery ball, and other trick deliveries were not all the batters had to worry about. Catcher Mike Kelly invented the cute trick of throwing his mask a few feet up the first-base line to trip a batter who had just connected solidly. And pitchers were not in the least bit shy about bouncing the ball off a batter's noggin. What the fans today would term dirty play was then viewed as just another part of the game.

Even Connie Mack, that paragon of virtue as a manager, was well known in the 1880's for his wiles as a catcher. When his team was at home, and thus responsible for supplying the baseballs, Mack would put several balls in the icebox overnight to deaden them. Each inning, when he came out to catch, he would give the sodden horsehides to the umpire to put in play— for the visiting-team batsmen, of course.

MOST FANS KNOW that the greatest base-stealer of the modern era is Ty Cobb, who stole 892 bases during his major-league career. And most fans know that Cobb's 96 steals in 1915 was the high-water mark until 1962, when Maury Wills pilfered 104.

What most fans don't know is that when it comes to larceny on the basepaths, Cobb and Wills must yield the spotlight to Harry Stovey and Billy Hamilton.

In 1888, Stovey stole 156 bases for a single-season record. Hamilton, a Hall-of-Famer, stole 937 bases in a 14-year career, 115 of them in 1891. "Sliding Billy," as he was called, also compiled a lifetime batting average of .344.

Caught in the Act

The Baltimore Orioles of 1894-96 were the best team baseball had seen up to that time, and the craftiest. Wee Willie Keeler, Hughie Jennings, John McGraw, et al. were not above a discreet violation of the rules—if such would win them a game. Perhaps the most famous of the Baltimore tricks is the one that backfired.

Prior to the start of a home game, Oriole outfielders would plant a few baseballs in strategic spots in the tall outfield grass. Balls hit up the alleys or down the lines which looked like sure extra-base hits were miraculously held to singles.

One day, however, an opposing batter drove a ball up the alley in left-center field. Two Baltimore men converged on the ball. The left-fielder snatched up the ball he had hidden in the grass, whirled, and tossed it back into the infield, holding the batter at first base in spectacular style. Unknown to the left-fielder, his partner in center field had been able to reach the batted ball, which he tossed back to the infield.

When the umpire saw two balls coming in to second base, he was not slow to act. He awarded the game to the visiting team by forfeit.

NINE MEN have hit four homers in a single game, most recently Willie Mays, in 1961. But of these nine, two must come in for special mention—Little Bobby Lowe and Big Ed Delahanty. Both accomplished the four-homer feat in the era of the dead ball.

Second-baseman Lowe hit his four-baggers in 1894, the only year he ever led the league in homers. On that memorable May 30, two of his four blasts came in the third inning.

Delahanty hit his four on July 13, 1896, on his way to his second home-run crown. By the way, Big Ed twice hit .400. He is the only man who ever won the batting title in *both* leagues.

The Price of Success

Boston outfielder Hugh Duffy completed the 1894 season with a batting mark of .438. Since no player had ever done any better—except in 1887, when walks were counted as base hits—Duffy figured he should get a healthy raise.

The penurious front office figured otherwise. But Duffy refused to play for the same salary he made in 1894, and thus became a holdout. The fight wore on until the 1895 season was about to open. At last, Duffy got his raise—$12.50 a month.

For his part of the wretched bargain, Duffy had to agree to serve as captain of the team, which meant paying for all lost equipment. At the end of the season, when Duffy had to cough up the dough, he realized he had been duped. The cost of replacing the equipment was far greater than the raise he had received. In effect, he had taken a pay cut for hitting .438.

24

Hot Potato

Though he was a premier base-stealer and batsman, Tommy McCarthy of the Boston Beaneaters would beat you any way he could. Bill Klem used to tell this one about how Tommy forced a rule change in the early 1890's.

At that time, the rule pertaining to a man on third about to tag up on a sacrifice fly stated that the runner could not leave the base until the fielder had possession of the ball. When a runner stood on third and a fly ball was hit to McCarthy, he would let the ball hit his glove, then bounce it from one hand to the other as he ran in toward the diamond. By the time Tommy gripped the ball securely, of course, he was too close to home for the runner to chance a dash for the plate.

YOU THOUGHT the 1962 Mets were bad? Sure they were—what else can you call a team that loses 120 games while winning only 40?

But the record books tell of a club that made the Mets look like world-beaters—the Cleveland team of 1899. That club set a record by dropping 134 games while winning only 20. Cleveland's percentage was an all-time nadir of .129.

The Dead-Ball Days

1901-1919

In 1901, baseball was yanked into the modern era when an ex-sportswriter named Ban Johnson, who had formed the American League the year before, declared war on the National League. He lured away many of the Nationals' top performers, and overnight established his circuit as a major league.

In the 1902 season, the fledgling American League proved conclusively that it was here to stay by drawing more fans than the National League. In 1903, the Boston Americans defeated the Pittsburgh Nationals in the first modern World Series.

In the first two decades of the century, baseball was a game of finesse and strategic play. Base stealing and bunting were primary offensive weapons, for the ball was so dead that hardly anyone could slug it into the stands.

During this period, 12 men led the league in homers with

fewer than 10 round-trippers. One of these strong hitters was Ty Cobb, who topped the American League in 1909 with nine circuit-blows. By modern standards, the Georgia Peach was certainly no slugger. But between 1907 and 1919, Cobb won the batting title 12 times, far more often than anyone else has.

Only one other hitter has ever dominated an era to such an extent—a young Boston player who often pitched against Cobb. After the 1919 season, the Red Sox traded this fellow named Ruth to the Yankees, and the dead-ball days were over.

One Last Chance

Pitcher Harley "Doc" Parker came up for a cup of coffee with the Chicago Cubs in three separate years. He never appeared in more than 10 games in a season, and his major-league record was 5-8 when the Cubs cut him loose in 1896.

Kinda makes you wonder why, five years later, the Cincinnati Reds had enough faith in Doc Parker's right arm to let him start a game. The Reds must have wondered, too, after the game was over. Parker allowed 26 hits and 21 runs, both major-league records for nine-inning futility.

Not surprisingly, that one game Parker hurled for the Reds in 1901 was his last in a big-league uniform.

TODAY A HOME-RUN HITTER'S chief requisite is power. But in the early 1900's, speed was of the essence. Playing in spacious ballparks before the advent of the lively ball, a batter could collect a round-tripper more easily if he lined the ball between the outfielders and then ran like hell.

In 1902, Pittsburgh third-baseman Tommy Leach won the National League home run crown with a grand total of six four-baggers. Not one of those swats went out of the ballpark.

King for a Day

Jay Justin (Nig) Clarke was a major-league catcher off and on between 1905 and 1920. In only one of those years did he play in as many as 100 games, and over a playing career of 506 games, he finished up with a lifetime batting average of .254.

Not much of a career, you say? Maybe not. But in July of 1902, when Clarke was a 20-year-old kid with Corsicana of the Texas League, he was the brightest star on the baseball horizon. In a game against Texarkana, Clarke came to bat eight times and hit eight home runs!

PITCHER JIMMY ST. VRAIN played only one year for the Cubs, but that was enough time for him to earn a dubious place in the annals of baseball.

Though a southpaw, Jimmy batted righthanded, and rarely managed so much as a loud foul. In a 1902 game against the Pirates, disheartened Cub manager Frank Selee half-jokingly suggested that St. Vrain might as well try batting lefthanded. The 19-year-old hurler took him at his word, and dug in on the unfamiliar right side of the plate.

Lo and behold, the rookie's bat found horsehide at last, and the ball dribbled out toward short. Determined to make the most of this rare opportunity to run out a hit, Jimmy put his head down and took off in a cloud of dust—toward third base!

The Iron Man

Your pitcher who has to be coddled with three or four days rest after every mound assignment just walks off to Union Headquarters when you mention the name of "Iron Man" McGinnity.

For that famous old pitcher was well nigh indestructible, and would have laughed down his pitching sleeve at today's crop of tissue-paper athletes. McGinnity could pitch day after day without any apparent strain.

In August of 1903, Joe McGinnity, wearing a Giant uniform, pitched three full doubleheaders. He won all six games!

In one of these encounters, McGinnity allowed only one run. In two others, he held the opposition to two runs. In another, he yielded three tallies. And one afternoon, carrying a twin pitching burden, Joe helped win a close one by stealing home with a vital run.

When Joe McGinnity was 54 years old, the Iron Man was still taking a regular turn on the mound for the Dubuque team in the Missouri Valley League.

Bobbles, Bungles, and Boots

The Chisox didn't look good in their game against the Tigers on May 6, 1903. In the course of nine innings, the Chicagoans made 12 errors to tie the record for fumbles.

The Detroiters didn't gloat. Two years before, on May 1, 1901, in a game between the same two teams, it had been the Tigers who first set the record by booting an even dozen chances.

And on May 6, 1903, as the Chicagoans were kicking 12 balls, the Tigers showed their sympathy by fouling up six plays on their own. That's 18 errors—the most by any two teams in one game!

JUNE 2, 1903 was a dismal day in Flatbush. On that day, the Dodgers played three games against the Pirates. "Dem Bums" dropped every one!

BACK IN 1903, in the first World Series between the upstart American League and the established National League, Pirate hurler Charles Louis Phillippe twirled five complete games!

In that inaugural classic, Deacon Phillippe pitched and won three out of the first four contests. But Pittsburgh lost the Series, as the Bostons swept the last four games. Each team used only three pitchers.

Cyclone on the Mound

The major-league career of pitcher Denton "Cy" Young covered a stretch of 22 years. From 1890 to 1911, Young hurled an epic

31

total of 906 games, more than any other starting pitcher. For his 22 years, Young averaged better than 23 winning performances per season. He won 511 games in all.

Cy hurled three no-hit no-run games, and in 1904, pitched the first perfect game of the modern era. Facing the Athletics, Young mowed down the batters as if they were straw men. He went on to rack up 23 consecutive innings without allowing a hit!

When 45-year-old Cy Young went to the mound for the last time, he pitched a whale of a game, only to lose 1-0. His opponent in that 1911 heartbreaker? A rookie by the name of Grover Cleveland Alexander.

The Unpredictable Rube

"Come and see Rube fan 'em out!" That inscription, splashed in huge painted letters on walls and sidewalks, was familiar to fans around the turn of the century. They knew who the artist was. He was a man who believed in advertising—self-advertising! He was advertising a long, gawky, easy-going, lefthanded pitcher named George Edward Waddell.

And Waddell wasn't boasting, for fan 'em out he did. Indeed, there are many who hold that the Rube was the game's greatest pitcher. Certainly he was one of its greatest personalities. He was front-page copy for years.

Came two o'clock of a day the great Rube was scheduled to pitch—no one would be much surprised if Waddell turned up missing. He might have decided to go off fishing. He might have donned a drum-major's shako and gone off to join a parade. Or he might have decided to chase the fire engines off to a blaze. Once a frantic search located him under the stands, shooting marbles with a bunch of kids!

Early in his career, when Rube was with the Pittsburgh Pirates, the team played an exhibition game in the South on Easter Sunday. Some yokel in the stands threw an egg at Waddell and hit him square on the noggin. Although Rube's cranium was the one spot where a guided missile would do least harm, he determined to show the fans just how good he was. So he instructed his seven teammates in the field to go have a seat on the sidelines, and then proceeded to strike out the side on nine pitches.

Great player though he was, few managers could put up with the Rube for long. He was fired from club after club. Either Rube went—or the manager's sanity. Only Connie Mack seemed to know how to handle this loony southpaw.

One afternoon in a crucial series, Waddell pitched and won the first game of a doubleheader. During the intermission, Mack promised the Rube a day off to go fishing, provided he won the second game. That bait was all Waddell needed. He mowed 'em down like sandlot kids, and then he streaked out of the park for his fishing trip.

Rube found one kindred soul on the Athletics—his battery mate, Ossie Schreck. Ossie roomed with him and became the partner in most of Waddell's escapades. Once Rube and Ossie stepped out for a big evening on the town. After hitting all the high spots, the two ballplayers drifted back to their hotel. Deciding that the evening was still young, they gathered their teammates to continue the celebration in their room.

Next morning, Rube awoke aching all over—in a hospital room. He was encased in rolls of bandages. Painfully turning his head, the Rube saw his pal, Ossie, anxiously hovering over the bed.

"Oh-h," groaned the battered hurler. "How'd I get here? Last I remember, we was up in our rooms having a few drinks with the boys. What happened?"

"Don'cha remember?" asked Ossie. "Long about midnight, you suddenly got the idea you could fly. A couple of the boys said you wuz nuts, so you got mad and said you'd show 'em. Next thing I knew, you had the window open and out you hopped flappin' your arms, just like a bird."

"Holy cow!" howled the Rube. "I coulda been killed. Why didn'cha stop me?"

"What!" exclaimed Ossie in a tone of righteous indignation. "And lose the hundred bucks I bet you could do it?"

One day, Rube stormed into Connie Mack's office and announced that he was not going to sign his next contract. Since Waddell was the team's mainstay, Mack was prepared to make some concessions. "What's up, Rube?" he asked. "You want more money?"

"Naw, the dough's O.K.," Waddell admitted. "But I don't sign no more contracts unless it says in there someplace that that roommate of mine don't eat no more crackers in bed."

To save money, the club often arranged for Waddell and Schreck to sleep in the same bed. Ossie Schreck had a habit of munching soda-crackers before going to sleep. Mack saw it Rube's way, and wrote a clause into Schreck's contract prohibiting him from eating his crackers in bed.

George Edward Waddell's major-league career was all too short because he never could beat old John Barleycorn. But at his best, few pitchers, if any, could offer anything to compare with his magic.

First Chance You Get—Hit 'im!

Frank Chance, star first-sacker of the oldtime Cubs, holds what is probably the most painful record in baseball.

On May 30, 1904, the Cubs played a doubleheader. During the first game, Chance was hit by the pitcher three times, a major-league record held by many.

Coming into the second game, the durable Frank was still standing. But the opposing pitchers were still on target, and Chance took two more direct hits—making a total of five free rides to first.

If there were a Purple Heart in baseball, Frank Chance would certainly have earned it.

IF YOU TOOK yourself to the ballgame in the first years of this century, your gustatory fancies were tickled not only by peanuts, crackerjacks, soft drinks, and ice cream, but also by cherry pie, cheese, chewing tobacco, chocolate, planked onions, and even tripe.

In addition to beer, hard liquor was available at most parks, but was eventually booted out of the stadia as the temperance movement grew in power.

Happy Jack's Sad Day

When a pitcher wins 20 games in a season, that's good. When a pitcher wins 20 or more games two seasons in a row, that's sensational. But when a pitcher wins 20 or more games twice in one season—that's real pitching!

And that's just what Jack Chesbro did in 1904, when they still called the boys from the Bronx the Highlanders. Out of 53 decisions for the New Yorkers that season, Chesbro won 41! No one in this century has won as many.

Tragically enough, Chesbro undid all his miracle work with a single pitch. In the final inning of the final game of the season, Happy Jack threw a pitch over the catcher's head, and a Boston runner scored from third. It cost New York the game—and the pennant.

THEY STILL call it the *Pitchers' World Series*. In 1905, the Philadelphians won only the second game, as Chief Bender hurled a shutout. The Giants swept the other four, 3-0, 9-0, 1-0, and 2-0.

And the big pitcher in this Pitchers' World Series was

Christy Mathewson. Big Six hurled three out of the four Giant shutout victories.

The Perfect Crime

Occasionally a baserunner can steal a base without sliding. But Fred Clarke, player-manager of the Pittsburgh Pirates, made the toughest theft of all: he stole home plate without even running!

It all happened in a 1906 game between the Pirates and the Cubs. Pittsburgh was at the plate. Bases were full, with Clarke on third. The count was three balls and one strike. The Chicago moundsman zipped one in, shoulder high. When the umpire uttered not a word and made no signal, Clarke assumed that the throw was high for ball four. That would automatically send him across for a run. Calmly, he left third base and ambled toward the plate. The batter, having heard nothing from the umpire and seeing Clarke walking in from third, came to the same conclusion. He tossed aside his bat and trotted toward first. This was enough to convince the catcher, who tossed the ball back to the moundsman and waited for the next batsman to step into the box.

As Clarke nonchalantly touched the plate, the arbiter suddenly came to life. "Strike two!" he shouted.

Jaws dropped. Everyone turned and stared at the umpire. "Frog in my throat," explained the embarrassed official. "Couldn't get a word out."

The batter returned to the plate. But since time had not been called, the game was officially on. The umpire was forced to rule that Clarke's run was valid. There was no other way for the scorer to write it up but as a stolen base.

Yes sir! Clarke had stolen home without the slightest intention of doing it!

The Hitless Wonders

The 1906 Chicago White Sox were one of the most amazing teams in baseball. There wasn't a .300 hitter on the entire squad. They wound up the season with a batting average of .228—the lowest in the league. Yet the Sox won the pennant, and went on to demolish a powerful Cub team in the World Series.

Along the way, the "Hitless Wonders" burned up the circuit with a 19-game winning streak. This is still the American League record, though tied by the 1947 Yanks.

The "Hitless Wonders" were really quite wonderful.

DURING ONE STRETCH of the 1906 season, the New York Highlanders—predecessors of the Yanks—put in plenty of overtime. They played five doubleheaders in five consecutive playing days.

The New Yorkers played twin bills against the Senators on August 30, August 31, and September 1. On September 3, they faced the Athletics in a two-gamer. Next day, the hard-working New Yorkers put in a double stint against Boston.

This overtime work paid off handsomely: The Highlanders won 10, lost none.

How to Succeed in Pitching Without Really Trying

Nick Altrock, now remembered as a great baseball clown, once turned in one of the strangest pitching performances ever recorded. Although he didn't pitch a single ball to any batter, Nick was credited with a win as the pitcher.

Here's how it happened: In the ninth inning of a game in 1906, Altrock went in as a relief hurler for the White Sox. The Chisox were one run in the hole. When Nick was summoned to the mound, there were two out and three men on. A moment after he took his place on the hill, Altrock threw to first, picking off the runner and retiring the side.

In their half of the ninth, the Chicagoans scored two runs to win the game. In the books, Nick Altrock went down as the winning pitcher, though he never tossed a single ball in the direction of the plate!

Trio of Bear Cubs, and Fleeter Than Birds

The most famous double-play combination of all time is undoubtedly Joe Tinker, Johnny Evers, and Frank Chance of the Chicago Cubs. This trio entered the Hall of Fame as a unit, though only Chance was a truly outstanding player. Indeed, their fame as a superior double-play combo is due principally to Franklin P. Adams' famous poem:

> These are the saddest of possible words—
> "Tinker to Evers to Chance."
> Trio of bear cubs, and fleeter than birds—
> "Tinker to Evers to Chance."
> Ruthlessly pricking our gonfalon bubble,
> Making a Giant hit into a double—
> Words that are weighty with nothing but trouble:
> "Tinker to Evers to Chance."

The fact of the matter is that in the four years from 1906 to 1909—the peak of their career—the vaunted trio completed only 54 twin killings—an average of less than 14 a year! Compare this to the 217 double plays completed by the Philadelphia A's in 1949 alone.

IN 1906, THE CUBS clawed their way through the National League with a vengeance.

At season's end they had won 116 games and lost only 36 for a sensational won-lost percentage of .763. This is the loftiest mark ever racked up by a club in either league.

The Gray Eagle

In 1908, the Boston Red Sox traded a rookie outfielder to Little Rock in exchange for the use of that minor-league team's spring-training field. Later that season, their faces as red as their socks, the Boston club hastily bought that player back! The rookie they had so casually palmed off as payment for a practice diamond was Tris Speaker—probably the greatest ballhawk in baseball history.

Anything from a Texas-Leaguer to a garden-wall clout was

duck soup for the great center-fielder. He patrolled a tremendous area, and not the least of his equipment was a magnificent left arm.

Speaker played a dangerously short center field—just a few yards behind the infielders. This always looked like a perfect set-up for a long-ball hitter. But Tris knew otherwise. At the first crack of wood against horsehide, the Gray Eagle would be off under full steam, going back, back, back. When the ball came down there was Tris, waiting to gather it in. His judgment was unerring; his instinct, uncanny.

The Gray Eagle was virtually a fifth infielder, for he stationed himself so close to second base that he was often able to field a grounder and throw the runner out at first.

Twice in one month Speaker completed an unassisted double play in this fashion: with a man on second, the batter hit a line drive up the middle for what looked like a run-scoring single. But as the runner on second hightailed it for third, Speaker raced in to intercept the ball before it dropped safely. Upon doing so, Tris simply trotted over to second base before the amazed runner could return to the bag.

But Tris' talents weren't confined to gamboling with a glove in the garden. He was a pretty handy fellow with the stick as well. In 22 years in the majors, Tris constructed a lifetime batting average of .344.

Speaker starred for the Red Sox from 1907 through 1915. In 1916, Tris went to Cleveland, where in 1919 he became player-manager. Under his tutelage, the Tribe won the World's Championship in 1920. His team was also runner-up for four seasons—a terrific record for the eight years Speaker ran the club.

A great sportsman, as well as a great player, the Gray Eagle was one of baseball's most beloved figures. He was one of the first players elected to the Cooperstown Hall of Fame.

Two Goose Eggs, Sunny Side Up

Here's an iron-man performance that will match any in the books.

On September 26, 1908, with the Cubs pounding down the

stretch in a nip-and-tuck three-way pennant race, Ed Reulbach was called upon to hurl both games of a crucial doubleheader with the Dodgers.

Not only did Reulbach pitch two full games, but he won both of them. Not only did he win them, he won both by shutouts!

What's more, Ed was going even better in the second game of the day, yielding only three hits in the nightcap.

IN 1908, WHEN Sir Walter Johnson was a green kid in his first full year with Washington, he set the pattern for future greatness. The Senators were playing a rough three-game series with the Yanks. The 20-year-old Johnson hurled the first game of the series on a Friday. He won by a shutout, allowing only six hits. On Saturday, the starting pitcher for Washington was Walter Johnson. He shut out the Yankees again, this time allowing the New Yorkers only four hits. There was no game on Sunday. On Monday, in the box for the Senators was—uh-huh—Walter Johnson. By this time the shutout habit was ingrained, and Johnson blanked the New Yorkers again. Only now, he cut their quota of safeties to two!

Here was the most astounding trio of triumphs ever won by any pitcher. Three games in four days—every one a shutout!

Only 12 hits for the three games! Are you listening, Frank Merriwell?

A Bonehead for Life

One of the smartest, heads-up ballplayers ever to wear a major-league uniform is remembered today by his wholly undeserved nickname of Bonehead Merkle. The nickname stemmed from one freak play.

The Giants, Pirates, and Cubs were bunched in a thrilling three-way race for the league lead in the closing weeks of the 1908 season. The Giants were at home at the Polo Grounds playing a crucial series against the Cubs. In his first full game of the season for the Giants, on September 8, 1908, Merkle was performing very creditably at first base.

Coming down to the last half of the ninth, the air-tight thriller was tied up at 1-1. With two down, Moose McCormick was on third and Merkle on first. Al Bridwell, Giant shortstop, was at bat. Bridwell came through, cracking a line-drive single into center field. McCormick romped home with the winning run.

Merkle, running between first and second, saw his teammate cross the plate. Fred abruptly left the basepaths and ran toward the dugout. He wanted to avoid the mob of jubilant New York fans who were already swarming out onto the field. There was nothing unusual about Merkle's act: the rookie was only doing what he had seen dozens of veteran big-leaguers do before him.

But amid the postgame confusion on the field, Johnny Evers, quick-thinking Cub second-baseman, stood on the keystone, screaming at his teammates to throw him the ball. When umpire Hank O'Day trotted over to find out what all the rumpus was about, Evers insisted on his calling Merkle out on a force play. He claimed that Bridwell had to get to first to qualify the hit, and if Bridwell must occupy first, then Merkle was forced to second. If, argued Evers, Merkle was out on the play, then of course McCormick could not have legitimately scored. There was much to-do for a long while, but finally O'Day had to yield to Evers' unimpeachable logic.

By this time, the crowd was at flood-tide on the field. There could be no question about resuming the game. With the score knotted at 1-1, the game was called. When the season finished two weeks later, the Cubs and Giants were in a tie for first place. In the single-game playoff, the Cubs triumphed, 4-2, winning the pennant.

Giant fans never recovered from their disappointment, and thereafter hung the moniker of "Bonehead" on a ballplayer who turned in 15 years of first-rate baseball.

Has Anyone Seen Home Plate?

On August 28, 1909, home plate was in its usual spot. But Bill "Dolly" Gray, Washington pitcher, couldn't seem to find it.

In the second inning of a game against the White Sox, Gray was as wild as a goose chase, yielding seven passes in a row. In

that one frantic frame, bounteous Bill donated a total of eight free rides.

Why didn't the manager remove him? Chances are he didn't want to kill a world's record.

BUGS RAYMOND, a pitcher for the New York Giants at the turn of the century, sat down to lunch. After taking his order, the waiter asked Bugs how he threw his spitball.

Rising from his chair, the clowning hurler picked up a water glass, wet two fingers, threw up his left leg, and sent the glass sailing through a window. "That's how it's done," he grinned. "And note the break!"

Giants manager John McGraw was not always amused by his pitcher's antics. One day, he had a few of his guards detain Raymond in the clubhouse to make sure the hurler would be in shape to pitch the second game of a doubleheader. Undaunted, Bugs lowered an empty bucket out the clubhouse window, and a confederate filled it with beer.

The Flying Dutchman from Pittsburgh

A Giant rookie about to face the Pirates once asked John McGraw how he should pitch to Honus Wagner. "Just throw the ball and pray," was McGraw's reply.

No cagier batter ever waved a stick at a pitcher than John Peter Wagner. He stood far away from the plate, at the extreme corner of the batter's box, and stepped into the pitch. He kept his hands far apart on the bat so he could place the hit where he wanted it, or bring his powerful hands together to take a full swing, if the pitch was a fat one.

For 17 consecutive years he batted over .300—winning the National League batting crown eight times, the best mark in the league's history.

But good as he was as a batsman, the Flying Dutchman was a shortstop *par excellence*. They haven't come much better.

He wasn't much to look at, this Wagner. Just about medium height, solid, and bandy-legged—but all muscles, and hands so huge you couldn't always tell whether or not he was wearing his glove. His legs were so bowed you might roll a barrel through them. *But never a baseball!*

Wagner could come up with a throw from any position—crouching, kneeling, or on the dead run. His peg, sidearm or overhand, always traveled with bullet speed and rifle accuracy. Many a time he brought the fans cheering to their feet by skipping nimbly into the short field behind third, spearing a sizzler that had eluded the third baseman, and slipping it to first in time for the putout.

Moreover, Honus studied the habits of players and seemed to be able to sense just where the ball was going to go. When it arrived anywhere near shortstop, you could be sure that the Flying Dutchman would be right on top of it.

On the basepaths, Honus was a greyhound. From a standing start on the far side of home plate, he once was clocked running the 30 yards to first base in 3.4 seconds.

A master of the stolen base, Wagner would bend his bandy legs into as slick a slide as baseball has ever seen. Time and again, the baffled baseman would reach down and tag nothing but dirt, only to find the Dutchman lying comfortably with his toe hooked securely around the sack.

Honus was sure a honey!

The Strangest Batting Race Ever

As the 1910 season wound down to a finale, Ty Cobb seemed to have a lock on the American League batting title for the fourth year in a row. In fact, Cobb was so far out in front of his nearest rival, Nap Lajoie, that he elected to sit out the final two games to protect his .384 average. He figured that Lajoie could not win the title, unless Cobb himself helped out by going 0-for-4 a couple of times.

The Chalmers Motor Car Company had announced that it would award its classiest auto to the winner of the batting title. Almost all American Leaguers would have preferred to see the car go to Cleveland's Lajoie, as popular a man as ever played the game. By contrast, Cobb was roundly hated for his rough style and arrogant manner.

On the last day of the season, Cleveland played a twin bill in St. Louis. To look at the box score, you'd think Lajoie had an amazing day. Eight official at-bats, eight hits—enough to bring his average up to .384. What the box score could not reveal was that of Lajoie's eight hits, six were bunt hits toward third, where a rookie was playing halfway into left field. One hit was a grounder on which the Browns' shortstop threw wildly to first; the official scorekeeper saw it as a safety. Only one hit was clean —a triple over the center-fielder's head.

Clearly, there was something rotten in St. Louis. An investigation ensued, and though no one was officially convicted of wrongdoing, neither the Browns' manager, Jack O'Connor, nor the third-base coach, Harry Howell, ever appeared on a big-league field again. The rookie third-baseman, Red Corriden, was exonerated since he had only been following orders.

For Lajoie, who had no part in the fix, and Cobb, everything came up roses. When their averages were computed more precisely, it emerged that Cobb had finished with a mark of .3848, while Lajoie closed with a .3841. Graciously, the Chalmers people gave each player a car.

The following year, however, Chalmers did not offer an automobile to the batting champ, but a plaque to the Most Valuable Player. A plaque is still awarded today, by the Baseball Writers Association of America.

Mack Gets His Money's Worth

Connie Mack had his Athletics play through two complete World Series without his making a change in the lineup during any one game! Not a relief pitcher, not a pinch-hitter, not a pinch-runner —the same men who started each game finished it.

Mack used a total of only 12 men during the five games of each Series.

Only two pitchers, Chief Bender and Jack Coombs, took the mound for the A's during the 1910 classic. In 1913, Mack had Bender, Eddie Plank, and Bullet Joe Bush alternate on the slab. What's more, the A's won each Series, four games to one.

Connie used to draft them for the duration!

So How Come "Home Run"?

They called him "Home Run" Baker. Yet John Franklin Baker, ace third-sacker of the Athletics, never hit more than 12 homers in any one season!

How come he got his name? Well, he hit them when they counted, and at a stage in baseball history when home runs were mighty scarce. Baker gained his fame in the World Series of 1911. The A's were pitted against a Giant team that had a terrific reputation. In the second game, the count was tied at 1-1 in the sixth inning. The Athletics had one on with two out. Baker came to bat.

Rube Marquard, the Giant hurler, slid one down the center. Wham! Baker's mighty bludgeon lifted the ball into the right-field stands.

For the rest of the game, the Athletics couldn't lay a bat on a ball for a safe hit. But they didn't have to. Baker's homer had put the game on ice by a score of 3-1.

Next day, Christy Mathewson faced the A's. Big Six was at the top of his form. For the first eight innings, the Athletics' scoreboard featured oval-shaped digits. Going into the ninth, the Giants held a slim 1-0 lead. With one down, Baker stepped to the plate to face the mighty Matty. You don't need three guesses to know what happened. Baker's home run tied the score, and paved the way for the Athletics' 11th-inning victory.

From that day on, John Franklin Baker was known as Home Run Baker. As the ditty goes, " 'Taint what you do, it's the way you do it."

Baker didn't connect with another four-bagger during the Series; and it wasn't until two years later that he slammed his best total of 12.

McGraw's Good Luck Charm

Early in the 1911 season, a tall, lanky man in a dark suit and black derby walked up to manager John McGraw while the Giants were taking batting practice. He informed the New York helmsman that, according to a fortune teller, if McGraw let him pitch for the Giants, they would win the pennant.

McGraw gave the daffy stranger a tryout, and quickly discovered he was strictly bush-league, if that good. Nevertheless, the superstitious McGraw, taking no chances, signed him on as a mascot.

For the rest of the season, at home or on the road, Charles "Victory" Faust would don a uniform and warm up before each Giant game. The fans took to the zany pitcher and clamored for McGraw to put him in a game. After the Giants had clinched the pennant, McGraw actually did send the mascot in for two short appearances.

The next year, Faust appeared at spring training, explaining that the Giants still needed him. That year he warmed up before every game, though he appeared in none, and once again the Giants went on to win the pennant.

In 1913, the mascot was once more with the club. By now a well-known baseball figure, Faust was signed for a brief vaudeville appearance. In the four days he was gone, the Giants dropped all four games they played. Convinced that the team could not win without him, Faust returned, and the Giants went on to win another pennant.

In 1914, "Victory" Faust was committed to a mental institution, thus depriving McGraw of his mascot. That year, the Giants failed to win the pennant.

To QUOTE a few old lines:

> *Breathes there a fan with soul so dead,*
> *Who never to the ump hath said,*
> *"Yer blind, you bum!"*

The answer is undoubtedly no. It's the accepted belief of the baseball fan that no umpire can even see the mask in front of his face.

But back in 1911, National League prexy Thomas Lynch, himself a former umpire, finally became fed up with these never-ending slurs. Accordingly, he appointed a committee of oculists to test the vision of every arbiter in the league. The report showed that every umpire had '20-20' vision or better—indeed, in most cases their visual acuity was far above average.

Has this scientific evidence silenced the critics? Yes—except for two words: "Oh, yeah?"

ONE SWALLOW doesn't make a summer, nor do three strikeouts always make an inning. Walter Johnson, Washington's great hurler, found that out on April 15, 1911, when he had to whiff four men to retire the side for keeps.

In the fifth inning of that day's game with the Red Sox, the Big Train fanned the batting order—one, two, three! But the Washington catcher dropped the last third strike, and the batter managed to reach first safely. So Johnson calmly proceeded to strike out the fourth man!

There was no appeal from that one.

Say It Ain't So, Joe

Joe Jackson earned the sobriquet "Shoeless Joe" because that's the way he played ball back home in the "hollers" of South Carolina. When the hillbilly came to the majors, he was still illiterate, but he had accustomed himself to wearing spikes on the field.

After a five-game trial with Connie Mack's A's in 1908 and another in 1909, Jackson was traded to Cleveland. The Naps, as they were then called, sent him to the minors for more polishing.

In 1911, Jackson finally got the chance to play every day. And what a rookie year he had! He fielded brilliantly and hit .408. In the nine years that followed, Shoeless Joe never hit below .300, and three times topped .370. His lifetime mark of .356 was bettered only by Ty Cobb and Rogers Hornsby.

Yet Shoeless Joe's name cannot be found on any plaque in the Hall of Fame. Though his playing credentials are certainly worthy of Cooperstown, Jackson was one of eight White Sox players who conspired with gamblers to throw the 1919 World Series.

On September 28, 1920, Jackson left the Cook County Courthouse after confessing to his role in that plot. As he walked down the steps, surrounded by photographers and newsmen, Jackson was accosted by a ragged little boy who pleaded, "Say it ain't so, Joe!"

But it was so, and Jackson went back to South Carolina in disgrace. He and the seven other "Black Sox" were banished from baseball for life.

ON SUCCESSIVE days in the 1911 World Series, Philadelphia A's third baseman John Baker hit home runs that were instrumental in defeating the New York Giants. Forever after, he was known as Home Run Baker.

Three decades later, along came another man who might have been called Home Run Baker. Over a 13-year span, infielder Floyd Baker came to bat 2,280 times and hit ony one four-bagger. There has never been a worse home-run hitter in major-league history.

Grand Larceny

When it comes to free-wheeling on the basepaths, no one has ever matched the record of Josh Devore, old-time Giant outfielder.

On June 20, 1912, in the ninth inning of a game against the Braves, Josh came up to bat. He reached first safely and then stole second. Then he went ahead and stole third.

That's pretty enough. But the New Yorkers had a terrific

inning, and batted all through the batting order. When Josh got up again, he repeated his entire performance.

That made a total of four stolen bases in one inning!

The Zaniest of Them All

With every ticket, the American baseball fan buys the privilege of razzing two managers, four umpires, and 18 ballplayers on the field beneath him.

In the early part of the century, Herman "Germany" Schaefer turned the tables. He gave the razzberry to the fans. And he always administered his chiding in the cleverest way.

Once, when Germany was playing second base for Detroit, the Tigers were appearing in Chicago in a game against the White Sox. The day before, Schaefer had bragged to newsmen what he was going to do to the Sox pitchers. That afternoon, he took a terrible riding from the Windy City supporters. The razzing grew louder and more gleeful the second time he was put out.

The third time Germany stepped up to bat, he held up his hand for silence. Turning to the stands he bellowed, "Ladeez and gentlemen! Pay close attention! You are about to witness a marvelous exhibition of the art of batting by the one—the only—the world's greatest hitter—Germany Schaefer!"

The hoots and catcalls that greeted this declaration were more thunderous than ever.

The first pitch was a strike. Germany merely bowed and announced, "That's one for the build-up!"

A second pitch came over. Strike two! Schaefer tipped his cap to the jeers and shouted, "That's just for suspense!"

On the third throw, Schaefer swung. The ball soared over the upstretched arms of the helpless Chicago left-fielder and into the stands for a home run.

Schaefer started to jog around the bases. As he touched first, he turned to the stands and yelled, "Schaefer beats it out to first!" Reaching second, he threw a hook slide, got up and shouted, "Schaefer gets to second before the ball!" Then he raced to third where he shouted, "Schaefer safe by a mile!" Germany then sprinted toward home base and raised the dust in a circus slide across the plate. Rising, he brushed himself off and addressed the fans again. "Ladeez and gentlemen!" he cried. "This concludes the great batting exhibition for this afternoon. Mr. Herman Schaefer, the world's greatest hitter, thanks you each and every one for your kind attention." Amidst laughter and applause, he tipped his cap and trotted off to the dugout.

Umpires, of course, were also subject to Schaefer's shenanigans. There was the time Schaefer, poised on third base, tried to make it across the plate on a long outfield fly. At the catch, he lit out for home. But when he arrived, the catcher was waiting for him with the ball. So was the ump with the classic thumb-in-the-air signal.

Schaefer rose from his futile slide and addressed the umpire. "I'm safe," he said. "I got here before the throw."

"Yuh did not," snapped the ump.

"When I hit home plate," claimed Schaefer, "I knocked the ball out of the catcher's mitt."

For answer, the umpire just pointed to the ball still clutched in the catcher's hand.

"I didn't feel him touch me. He musta missed the tag."

"He did not," growled the ump. "He got you all right."

At this point, Schaefer turned and faced the stands. "Ladeez and gentlemen!" he shouted, "Can anybody think of any more excuses? I'm plumb out of them myself!"

Another time, with Detroit playing the Indians, Schaefer tried to induce the ump to call the game on account of rain. It was the top half of the fifth. At the time, Cleveland was winning 5-1. If the game were called before four and a half innings had been played, the game would have been declared no contest. But the umpires insisted that the game go on. When Detroit took the field in the sixth, Schaefer with great dignity strode to his place at second base wearing a long raincoat. He played through the inning dressed like that. At the end of the sixth inning, the game was officially washed out with the Indians in the lead 6-1.

Perhaps his most famous antic was the time Schaefer, perched on second, stole first base. It was back in 1911. Schaefer was playing for Washington in a game against the White Sox. Going into the ninth, the game was tied. There were two out and two on for Washington. Schaefer was on first. Clyde Milan, a blue streak on the basepaths, was poised at third. A single run would be decisive, but a weak hitter was coming to the plate.

On the first pitch, Schaefer dashed down to second. The Sox catcher didn't even try for him. On the next pitch, Germany startled everybody by sprinting back to first base, hooking the bag with a dramatic slide. The play, of course, was a smoke-screen. Germany's idea was to draw a throw from the catcher, and thus allow Milan to get home from third in the confusion.

The strategy failed. The catcher held on to the ball. Schaefer succeeded, however, in creating confusion—at least among the umpires.

The White Sox stormed onto the field in protest. This so-and-so was making a travesty of the game. On what base was he, anyhow?

The arbiters went into a huddle with the Book of Rules. No one had anticipated such a loony play. They could find nothing in the rules about a player not being able to steal in reverse. The play was allowed.

Then Germany came right back and stole second again! This time, Milan came in to score as the throw went down to second. Soon all was tranquil, except that the scorer was still in a state of mild hysteria on how to score the play.

As a ballplayer, Schaefer broke no records—but he did split sides.

Spicy Spitter

The last of the spitball pitchers has allegedly vanished from the major leagues, and the saliva delivery is now banned by the rules. But in the spitballer's heyday, the unpredictable behavior of the moistened pitch had many a batter gnashing his teeth. Fred Luderus, first-sacker of the Phillies, found one answer to the problem. He fought water with fire!

It was in a 1912 game against the Pirates' Marty O'Toole, a very effective spitball pitcher. O'Toole's moistening technique was to hold the ball up to his face and lick it directly with his tongue. Then he would wind up and send the dampened pill on its eccentric course to the plate.

When the Phillies took the field, Luderus carried in his back pocket a tube of liniment. Every time the ball came his way, the first-baseman would rub a little of the fiery ointment into the horsehide. (In those days, a single ball might stay in play for a full nine innings.) Before the third inning was over, O'Toole's tongue was so raw and inflamed he had to be taken out of the box.

Manager Fred Clarke of the Pirates squawked to high heaven. He protested that the use of the liniment was illegal, a threat to eyesight, peace of mind, and the Constitution.

But Charlie Dooin, Phillie manager, indignantly rejected Clarke's protests. "I ordered Luderus to do it to protect my boys," he proclaimed self-righteously. "Why, that nasty habit of O'Toole's was putting millions of germs on every pitch."

"And," he concluded, "every time O'Toole spits on that ball, we're going to disinfect it. There's nothing in the rules that says we don't have the right to protect our health!"

And there isn't!

The Sit-Down Strike

On May 15, 1912, the Detroit Tigers were playing the New York Yankees at the Polo Grounds. Ty Cobb was being heckled incessantly by one fan in the grandstand, and as the game wore on, the Georgia Peach's patience wore exceedingly thin. He asked the New York manager to do something, since crowd control was the responsibility of the home team. But this particular fan continued to malign Cobb's play, his lineage, and his manhood.

At last, not able to listen to another word of abuse, Cobb leapt into the stands and began to furiously pummel his tormentor. By the time police and spectators intervened, the erstwhile heckler was a bruised and bloody mess.

American League President Ban Johnson read the umpires' report of the incident, fined Cobb $100, and suspended him for 10 days. Although Cobb was perhaps the least liked man in baseball—even by his teammates—the Tiger players rallied to his support. Either Cobb played, the Tigers said, or they didn't.

Johnson ignored this threat and forced a showdown. The Tigers were due to play the Athletics in Philadelphia on May 18. If Detroit could not field a team on that date, Johnson said, they would have to pay a $5,000 fine to the league.

Detroit Manager Hughie Jennings pleaded with his men, but to no avail. They would not play without Cobb. On the morning of the game with the A's, Jennings signed up nine youths from St. Joseph's College and the Philadelphia sandlots—Bill Leinhauser, Dan McGarvey, Billy Maharg, Jim McGarr, Pat Meany, Jack Coffey, Hap Ward, Ed Irwin, and Aloysius Travers. All nine recruits played that afternoon, aided by two fortyish Tiger coaches who returned to active duty for the day.

The game was a horror, as pitcher Travers was belted for 24 runs. It wasn't all his fault, though, because nine errors by his mates led to 10 unearned runs. The fans who paid to see this game may have been bilked, but the Tiger management had saved itself five grand.

At Cobb's behest, the regular Tigers returned to the field next day. The nine instant major leaguers were paid and released. Only one ever donned a major-league uniform again: Billy Maharg, who four years later made another one-day stand, this time with the Phillies.

Strangely, nothing was ever heard again of Ed Irwin, who was the Tiger catcher on the day of the strike. He belted out two triples in three times at bat, and thus ended his big-league career with a batting average of .667.

The Dentist's Debut

Late in 1912, the Brooklyn Dodgers called up from the Montgomery, Alabama club of the Southern League a kid named Charles Dillon Stengel, a sometime dental student who hailed from Kansas City, Missouri. When Stengel arrived at the old Brooklyn ballpark on Washington Street, manager Bill Dahlen told him that he would play center field that day against Pittsburgh. And what a day it turned out to be!

On Stengel's first trip to the plate, Casey—as he came to be known—disregarded Dahlen's bunt sign, and singled to right-center. When Stengel came back to the bench, the manager asked him whether he had missed the sign.

"No," said Casey, "I saw it, but when the first pitch bounced in the dirt, I switched off on the next one. That's the way we did it down South."

"Listen, kid," said Dahlen. "I don't want you to carry too much responsibility. So why don't we say that I'll run the team and all you'll have to worry about is fielding and hitting."

The rookie's ears were bright red as he trotted out to center field. But Dahlen's chastening did not hurt Casey's play. He slammed three hits on his next three times at bat, and stole two bases.

When he came up for the fifth time, Pittsburgh manager Fred Clarke hollered, "All right, phenom, let's see you cross over." So Stengel stepped across the plate and assumed a right-handed stance. The pitcher was so flabbergasted that he walked the rookie. Casey's first day in the big time had been just perfect!

LIGHTNING ON SPIKES! That was Eddie Collins, great American League second-baseman. Eddie not only stole bases, he hijacked them in carload lots.

On September 11, 1912, Eddie was playing for the A's against Detroit. In that game, he pilfered six sacks.

Just to make this record doubly impressive, Collins duplicated the feat 11 days later against the St. Louis Browns.

Other base runners might be left holding the bag—but never Eddie Collins!

From Lemon to Limelight

Back in the days when a nickel would buy a good cigar and a thousand dollars would get you a bang-up ballplayer, the Giants paid the unheard-of sum of $11,000 for a rookie named Rube Marquard.

In his first few seasons, the bony lefthander was a flop of the first water. "The $11,000 Lemon," they called him.

But in 1912, Marquard astounded the baseball world by pitching and winning 19 straight ballgames! The marvelous Rube beat every club in the league at least twice, and shellacked Boston and Philadelphia four times each!

Under today's rules, Rube would have been credited with 20 wins. In one game, he relieved Jeff Tesreau when the Giant pitcher was a run behind. The Giants won, but under 1912 rules, Tesreau was credited with the victory.

Still, 19 straight victories in one season is a target for any pitcher to shoot at. No one since has found the range.

Pardon Me, Mayor...

By the 1910's, the custom of having an official throw out the first ball was established as part of opening-day ceremonies. During one such afternoon in Boston, the Mayor himself was on hand to put the ball in play. An ardent Braves fan, His Honor got the game underway, then took his seat to cheer his team on.

As the game progressed, Giant second-baseman Larry Doyle was spoiling the festivities with his fancy stickwork. The Boston fans were riding him hard, and the Mayor's voice was the loudest among them. When some of Hizzoner's more personal remarks reached Laughing Larry's ears, he charged the Mayor's box and angrily warned him to watch his tongue.

Caught up in the excitement, the Guest of Honor resumed his taunts the next inning. Finally, his patience taxed beyond endurance, Doyle rushed the box, pushed a few spectators aside, and punched his distinguished heckler in the jaw.

A brawl ensued, and Doyle was carted away to jail. Through it all, the Mayor of Boston slept soundly, out cold on the floor of his box.

A Relic at 27

When pitcher Joe Wood was called up to the Boston Red Sox in 1908, the righthander from Kansas was a tender 18 years. Yet Smokey Joe proved he could make the grade in the big time. Within a few years he had established himself as the premier hurler of the Bosox.

In 1912, his fifth year with the club, Joe won 16 consecutive games—an American League record—on his way to an overall mark of 34-5. He led his club to the pennant, and won three games in the World Series. A mere 22 years old, Smokey Joe could see only gold ahead.

But the following spring, Joe broke his thumb fielding a ground ball. When the cast was removed and he tried to pitch, his shoulder began to ache. Joe struggled to win 11 games in 1913, pitching with great pain. Two years later, he somehow managed to lead the league in ERA with a mark of 1.49.

Still, it was plain to see that Smokey Joe had lost his zip. His arm was so tender that sometimes he needed a couple of weeks after a start to even lift his throwing arm. Finally, in 1915, Joe called it quits and returned to Kansas.

But after nearly two years at home, the peace and quiet was too much for Joe to bear. He'd always been a good hitter and fielder, and decided to ask for a tryout with the Cleveland Indians, now managed by his old Boston buddy, Tris Speaker. In 1918, when Wood served the Tribe as an outfielder, he was considered a relic, a great from another day. Joe Wood was then all of 27 years old.

Yet Joe went on to play six years with the Tribe, once batting .366.

Always in Control

When Christy Mathewson was invited to West Point to give the cadets some pointers on pitching, he laid particular stress upon the matter of control. Somehow his confident remarks nettled one of the officers, and prompted a bet that Matty couldn't demonstrate the exact control he was prating about. Matty was to stand in the pitcher's box and throw 20 balls into the pocket of a stationary catcher's mitt propped up behind home plate. The bet also stipulated that at least three balls were to be curved deliveries.

Matty won.

During the 1913 season, the Giant ace hurled 68 consecutive innings without walking a man—a record that stood for nearly half a century. In that season, Matty pitched to 1,195 batsmen. In 306 innings, he walked a total of only 21 men. Against Big Six, a batter had to earn his way to first base.

Seventeen years in the big time, Matty became one of the immortal 14 pitchers who have won over 300 games. Matty won 373, to be exact, and compiled a lifetime winning percentage of .665.

For 12 seasons in a row, Matty won 20 or more games. For three straight seasons, he won 30 or more. In 1908, the great Matty pitched the Giants to 37 victories.

Mathewson owns the greatest World Series pitching record of all time. In the 1905 classic, Big Six hurled three games against the Athletics, and won every one by a shutout! No wonder Connie Mack said, "It was a pleasure to watch Mathewson pitch—when he wasn't pitching against you."

ON JULY 25, 1913, Carl Weilman of the Browns was nothing if not consistent. In the course of a 15-inning game against the

Senators, Weilman struck out six times. More recently, three other men have suffered the same embarrassment: Don Hoak of the Cubs in 1956; Rick Reichardt of the Angels in 1966; and Billy Cowan of the same team in 1971.

ON JUNE 6, 1913, Rabbit Maranville, playing for the Braves against the Cubs, tried three times to steal a base, and on each attempt was convicted of larceny. A perfect peg from Chicago catcher Jimmy Archer nabbed him in the act each time.

That day, the celebrated Rabbit was just another bunny in the hutch.

And Boo to You, Bill Klem!

In 1913, the Pirates and the Giants were locked in a decisive series. Calling them behind the plate was Bill Klem, an umpire who demanded—and commanded—plenty of respect. It was a close contest. Nerves were on edge. The Pirates were giving tough old Bill Klem as much guff as they dared.

Klem was slowly building to a blowup. Toward the end of the game he erupted, and stalked over to the Pirate dugout. "Listen, you guys," he exploded, "I've taken just about enough. Any more razzing from you and I clear the bench. Get it?"

By their stricken silence, the Pittsburgh players indicated that they got it, all right. Klem strode back to the plate and re-adjusted his mask and chest protector. Next man to step into the batter's box was a rookie, sent in by manager Fred Clarke as a pinch-hitter. The kid was so nervous that when he mumbled his name to Klem, Bill didn't hear it.

"C'mon now," barked Klem, "don't delay the game. Give me your name and be quick about it!"

The youngster swallowed fearfully and opened his mouth. "Boo!" he said hoarsely.

Klem blew his top. "That does it," he yelled. "You're out of the game. Get off the field!"

The abashed rookie retired to the bench in confusion. After a whispered consultation, Fred Clarke dashed onto the field to explain to the glowering Klem that the youngster, brand-new to the majors, had meant no offense. His name was Everett Booe!

BASEBALL OWNERS made a large portion of their annual profit from such ancillary sources of income as concessions, scorecards, and advertising space on the outfield fences. Capitalists clamored for the opportunity to publicize their wares before the ballpark audience, and many were clever enough to link their product with the hometown team.

For example, one ad taken out in Brooklyn's Ebbets Field read: "Zack Wheat caught 400 flies last season; Tanglefoot fly paper caught 10 million."

Baseball on Broadway

In the early days, off-season employment was quite a problem for most ballplayers. Many took to such menial tasks as hauling ice or delivering coal, for poor education prevented most players from gaining more lucrative employment. But for the stars of the game, there was one unfailing source of off-season money: the stage.

Few players had any talent. Some delivered monologues about "inside baseball"; others danced; still others did imitations; and a few even sang.

Ty Cobb once played the hero in a melodrama called *College*

Widow. Rube Waddell and Bugs Raymond, two of the nuttiest ballplayers ever, teamed in a potboiler named *Stain of Guilt*. And Christy Mathewson cleared $1,000 a week for appearing in a skit called "Curves" along with his batterymate Chief Meyers, and the popular actress May Tully. Charlie Dooin sang with Dumont's Minstrels in Philadelphia. In 1912, four Red Sox formed a passable quartet in Beantown. Joe Tinker did a baseball skit called "A Great Catch."

Rabbit Maranville took the stage as a baseball lecturer. Once, while demonstrating the art of stealing second base, Maranville slid with so much feeling that he flew over the footlights and bounced into a snare drum, spraining his ankle rather badly.

But the most successful of all the player-entertainers was "Broadway Mike Donlin, the Beau Brummel of Baseball," as he was called by *Vanity Fair*. Mike was a .334 lifetime hitter, but it was his dancing that "brought down the house," according to the New York *World*. The *Globe* declared that Donlin's act "created a small pandemonium of uproar," and *Variety* wrote that "if you miss him, you do yourself an injustice."

Donlin began to take so much stock in his press clippings that in 1909, he turned down the Giants' offer to play and stayed on the stage for the next two years.

In 1911, he returned to the diamond, and again hit over .300, but after 1914 he returned to Broadway for keeps. Then Donlin went on to make a few movies.

Maximum Efficiency

Today, baseball is a flashy, streamlined game, with plenty of slugging to drive runners around the bases.

But years back, a baserunner had to rely on his own two legs —and not so much on the bats of his teammates. If you couldn't smack the logy ball for extra bases, at least you could try to steal them.

When it came to steady year-in-year-out larceny, no major-league player except the fabulous Cobb has ever approached Pittsburgh outfielder Max Carey. For ten years between 1913 and 1925, Carey led the National League in stolen bases.

The downward motion of the pitcher's arm was the *Go* signal for Max. He could take off like a scared jackrabbit, and be down at the next way-station almost before the bewildered catcher could get the ball away. In 1922, he stole safely 51 times out of 53 attempts.

No indeed! You couldn't be lax with Max.

THE LONG ARM of the law had nothing on the long arm of Yankee catcher Leslie G. Nunamaker. In one inning, catcher Nunamaker nipped three runners trying to steal second.

On August 3, 1914, the Yanks were playing Detroit. The first three Tigers got on base. But thanks to Nunamaker's rifle arm, they didn't get very far. Three pegs—three outs! For a catcher, that's really pitching!

Bottoms Up!

They called them The Miracle Braves, and they called their manager, George Stallings, The Miracle Man. For only a miracle, it seemed, could hoist that dismal team from its cellar-spot to the top of the league.

On July 11, the Braves were dragging along 11½ games

behind the pace-setting Giants. But suddenly, the Boston team ate spinach and from there on, went on to win 59 of the next 75 games.

This last-to-first march was climaxed by a brilliant World Series victory over the Athletics—odds-on favorites to win the title. The A's were powered by their famous "$100,000 infield" and boasted one of the greatest pitching staffs of all time: Bender, Plank, Pennock, Shawkey, and Bush.

But The Miracle Braves laughed off all the dope. Connie Mack's supermen proved very vincible before the brilliant pitching of Rudolph, James, and Tyler. This trio allowed the titans from Philly exactly six runs in four games, as The Miracle Braves swept the Series.

On June 23, 1915, Bruno P. Haas made what is probably the most inauspicious pitching debut in big-league annals.

A schoolboy fresh from Worcester Academy, Haas was pitching for the Athletics against the Yanks. In nine raucous innings, Haas yielded 16 bases on balls—a major-league record. To make his parents even more proud, Bruno unleashed three wild pitches. His teammates soon caught the spirit of the day and contributed six errors to the afternoon's fun.

The Yanks spent a pleasant June afternoon strolling around the bases. The scorekeeper counted 15 tallies.

Grounder Defies Gravity

In 1916, George Cutshaw, Dodger second-baseman, broke up a ballgame with a ground ball that miraculously climbed over the fence for a home run!

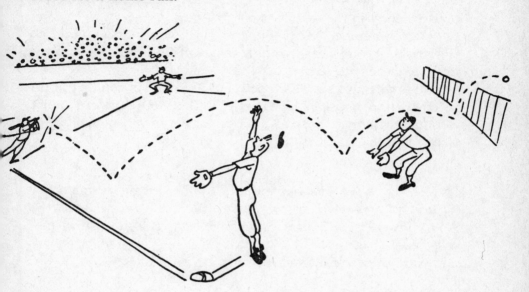

The Dodgers were playing the Phillies at Ebbets Field in a hard-fought, extra-inning game. With the score tied in the last half of the eleventh, Cutshaw slammed a hot grass-clipping drive into right field—a hard-hit ball worth two bases in any league.

But Cutshaw's grounder was marked for high destiny. As the Philadelphia right-fielder charged in to field the ball off the fence, the spheroid struck the embankment, and instead of caroming off the fence, continued to roll upward—urged on by some sort of English. The ball actually climbed the fence.

For a moment, the ball teetered at the top as if to taunt the Phillie fielder, and then it hopped over.

The Dodgers won the game. Cutshaw's smash has gone down in baseball history as the only ground ball that ever rolled outside a major-league ballpark. And in those days, a ball that cleared the fence on however many bounces was a homer, not a ground-rule double.

The things that can happen in Brooklyn!

Streaking Off to Nowhere

In 1916, the Giants rocketed to two sensational winning streaks. In May, they snapped back from an eight-game losing streak to win 17 in a row—all on the road. Then they came back home and coasted along in the middle of the NL pack.

On September 7, something touched off the fuse again. The Giants shot off to a new winning streak of 26 in a row—the all-time major-league record.

Yet with two such high-powered drives, they couldn't finish better than fourth place. The next year, the McGrawmen couldn't work up a winning streak all season, but they won enough games to cop the pennant.

IN 1916, THE A's power-dived into the American League cellar by losing 20 games in a row. Just to show it wasn't a freak, the A's repeated in 1943, once again hitting the skids for 20 successive losses.

Connie Mack sure learned how to take it.

Gorgeous George Sisler

In 1911, in a seven-inning practice game between the freshmen and the varsity at the University of Michigan, the frosh pitcher turned in a creditable performance. He fanned 20 of the 21 batters who faced him.

The Michigan coach, a fellow by the name of Branch Rickey, was somewhat impressed. Shortly afterward, when Branch was hired to manage the St. Louis Browns, he contacted the young southpaw and asked him to don a big-league uniform. George Harold Sisler was the way he endorsed his checks.

When Sisler rose to take his first time at bat in the big time, there were two men on base. Young George picked out a club and turned to Rickey asking, "Where'll I hit it, coach?" The veteran ballplayers in hearing distance were so astonished at the rookie's naive confidence, they couldn't even guffaw. But Rickey merely grinned and said, "Try the right-field fence, son." And that's where the ball went!

Good as Sisler was as a pitcher, the Browns could not afford to leave that kind of hitting out of the daily lineup. So one day Rickey told George to play first base exclusively.

How right Rickey was! George Sisler seemed to have been born to become the nonpareil first-sacker of his day. Twice Sisler hit over .400. In 1920, Sisler made what is still an unequaled record of 257 hits in a single season. In 1922, he slugged out a robust .420 and was named the Most Valuable Player of that season.

In 1939, Sisler was named to baseball's official Hall of Fame. Every oldtimer who ever saw George Sisler play was filled with pride by the selection. The Cooperstown solons had picked George as one of their first three first-basemen—along with Cap Anson and Lou Gehrig. And many believe that Sisler was the greatest of them all.

Aerial Bombardment

Gabby Street was known for once catching a ball dropped from the top of the Washington Monument. Not to be outdone, Dodger manager Wilbert Robinson, a former backstop himself, announced that he would attempt to catch a ball dropped from an airplane. The arrangements were made, and the players gathered around as Robbie stood with a mitt in the center of the spring-training diamond at Clearwater, Florida.

The big moment arrived. The plane flew overhead, and Uncle Robbie braced himself for the catch as the sphere came down. But the player up in the plane had substituted an enormous grapefruit for the baseball. It landed on top of Robbie's head with a tremendous thud and splattered all over him.

Momentarily knocked clear out of his senses, Robinson dropped to the turf. When he came to, he looked up at the concerned faces of the players and murmured, "I'd have caught that ball for sure if there hadn't been that damn cloudburst."

LEGEND HAS HAD IT that Edd Roush, a great outfielder for years with the Reds and the Giants, learned to throw with his left arm only after some mishap in his youth had deprived the right of its power. But the fact of the matter was that Roush's left arm was always stronger than his right.

As a boy, Edd had to throw with his right arm because there were no lefty gloves to be borrowed from his friends. Roush continued to throw with his right arm until he turned professional and could afford to buy his own glove. It was then he unveiled his lefty shotgun.

WHEN OLDTIMERS start batting the breeze in the hot-stove league, someone is sure to bring up the phenomenal shutout record of Grover Cleveland Alexander. Pitching for the mediocre Philadelphia Phils in 1916, Alex really dished up the goose eggs in wholesale lots. That year, he hurled 33 victories for the feeble Phillies —and of these, 16 were shutouts!

One year earlier, Alexander won 31 games for the Phils. In four of these, he allowed but a single hit.

No, there haven't been many who could match the cunning of Ol' Pete's right arm.

In the Land of the Blind, the One-Eyed Is King

Grim, bluff George Moriarty was calling them behind the plate. A big-league rookie stepped up to bat and watched a fast one go by. "Stri-i-ke one!" cried Moriarty.

The batter just glanced at the ump. The next pitch was another called strike.

This time the youngster turned to the man in blue. "Just for my information, sir, how do you spell your name?" he asked.

Caught off guard, Moriarty spelled out his name.

"That's what I thought, sir," said the ballplayer, stepping back into the batter's box. "Moriarty—with only one *i*."

Misery Loves Company

Here's a Rube Marquard feat in reverse. Johnny Nabors cops the honors. During the 1916 season, Nabors hurled for the Athletics. Connie Mack must have been awfully short of pitchers, because he had Nabors in there again and again, even though Nabors developed the losing habit to the point where it became an instinct.

Nabors went to the mound 40 times and compiled a won-lost record of 1-21. Nineteen of his losses came in succession. We don't know whether Connie Mack was obstinate or Nabors persistent. But apparently neither could be easily discouraged.

Philadelphia finished the 1916 season with 117 losses, a record only the New York Mets could break. Contributing mightily to this woeful performance was Nabors' roommate, Clancy Sheehan, who won one game while losing 15. Together, the roommates compiled a scintillating won-lost percentage of .052.

WHILE ON A ROAD TRIP, Dodger manager Wilbert Robinson was awakened in his hotel room at 1 A.M. by a loud knock on his door. Robinson angrily opened the door, and there stood a kid who had just come up from the bush leagues.

"I'm sorry, sir," the rookie said, "but they told me that when I joined the club here in Chicago, I should report to you immediately. Well, my bus just got in."

"I'll tell you what," the weary Uncle Robbie said with a devilish smile. "I want you to go and knock on every door on this floor and introduce yourself to the team."

Three quarters of an hour later, the young man was back at Robinson's door.

"Well?" said Robbie.

"I tried every door, sir," the rookie replied. "But nobody's in yet."

The Ultimate Pitchers' Duel

Anything you can do, I can do better—that's what Cincinnati pitcher Fred Toney seemed to be saying to his mound rival, Hippo Vaughn of Chicago. Inning after inning, Vaughn set down the Reds without a hit. Inning after inning, Toney treated the Cubs with similar disdain. On this 2nd day of May, 1917, the 3,500 fans in Chicago's Weeghman Park were being treated to a pitcher's duel without parallel.

In the top of the ninth, the lefthanded Vaughn set down the Reds to complete his no-hitter. What he needed now was a run. But the Cubs still couldn't even get a hit, as Toney completed *his* no-hitter.

In the top of the tenth, Red shortstop Larry Kopf drove a clean single to right, and after an error sent Kopf to third, Jim Thorpe hit a swinging roller down the third-base line. Vaughn had no play to first on the speedy Olympic hero, so he threw home to try to catch Kopf. But the Cub catcher, Art Wilson, was looking off toward first base, expecting Vaughn's throw to go there. When Hippo's throw arrived at the plate, it hit Wilson smack in the chest, and the run was in.

Toney had no trouble retiring the demoralized Cubs, and won his no-hitter. After losing the heartbreaker, all Vaughn could say in the clubhouse was, "Well, it's just another game."

But it wasn't. There has never been another to match it.

One, Two, Three, and Out

In 1918, Harry Heitman made his major-league debut with the Brooklyn Dodgers. Manager Wilbert Robinson gave Harry the ball and pointed him toward the mound. The rookie gave a single to the first man he faced, a triple to the next, and another single to the next—whereupon the manager's patience with the youngster was tried beyond endurance. Uncle Robbie took the ball back, and pointed his pitcher toward the clubhouse.

Heitman proceeded to shower, dress, and leave the ballpark. He went straight to a Navy recruiting station, enlisted, and never played ball again.

ON SEPTEMBER 28, 1919, the Giants and the Phillies met in a real quickie. From the umpire's *Play Ball!* to the final putout was a matter of less than an hour. In jig-time, the Giants managed to put together six runs to win 6-1.

It was a full nine-inning contest. Each team made the requisite number of putouts. No baseball commissar stood by with a whip to enforce the Stakhanovite speed-up.

The Georgia Peach

For nearly a quarter of a century, Ty Cobb dominated baseball. He could do practically everything better than anybody else. He was probably the greatest batter that ever lived, compiling a lifetime average of .367 over a period of 24 years of active and continuous play. In that long stretch of time, only in his abbreviated first season did Cobb's average fall below the .300 mark. From 1907 through 1915, the Georgia Peach was the undisputed batting champion of the American League.

In 1916, Cobb was beaten out by the redoubtable Tris Speaker—despite the fact that Cobb hit .371 that year. But there was still plenty of power left in those muscles. The very next year, Cobb again clouted his way to the title which he held through 1919.

Cobb's record is all the more remarkable because it was compiled in the days when the ball was not stuffed with a jackrabbit. With the ball as slow as molasses, Cobb in 1911 managed to ring up the amazing average of .420. That was only one of three times he batted over .400.

And when Cobb got on base—which was often—the opposing team would be seized with a collective heart attack. On the paths, the Georgia gadfly was a ball of fire. Fleet as a fox, primed like a pointer, and cagey as a cat, Ty Cobb scored from first on singles, and hoofed it to the plate from second on sacrifice flies. Throughout his memorable career, Ty stole 892 bases.

Cobb didn't have to hit home runs. He could and did make a single do the work of a four-bagger. It is recorded that on three different occasions, Cobb got on first—and then proceeded to steal second, third, and home!

Ty Cobb was a terror on the bases in more ways than one. He was of the rough, tough school who believed that the basepaths belong to the baserunner, and let the baseman beware.

Cobb was a fighter. He played every game as though his life depended on it. But friend and foe alike averred that here was a man who could play baseball—the king of them all.

The Ruthian Era
1920-1935

Baseball entered the roaring '20s with a painful rush. Late in the 1920 season, it was revealed that eight Chicago White Sox players had conspired with New York gamblers to throw the 1919 World Series to Cincinnati.

But perhaps the most important event of the year 1920 was the introduction of the lively ball. The manufacturers of baseballs for the American League switched from American yarn to a stronger, tighter Australian variety. This subtle change may have helped Babe Ruth—then in his first year with the Yankees—to clobber 54 homers, nearly twice as many as had ever been hit before.

In 1926, the lively ball was made still more lively as the cushioned cork center was approved for play. The following year, Ruth hit 60 homers to establish a new record and Murderers' Row clobbered all competition.

But the Yankee reign was brief, as Connie Mack's A's took

the spotlight from 1929 to 1931. The Bronx Bombers revived in 1932, but they were no longer the team they were in the '20s. Public attention soon shifted to St. Louis, where the Dean boys and Pepper Martin were ushering in the Gashouse Gang.

On May 23, 1935, the first night game in baseball history was played in Cincinnati's Crosley Field. Most observers regarded the experiment as a freakish promotional stunt, if not blasphemy. Few men realized that baseball's good old days were nearing an end.

Also nearing an end in 1935 was the career of the man who had personified baseball since 1920. Forty years old and fast fading, the Babe was playing out his string with the Boston Bees. Two days after the night game in Cincinnati heralded a new era, Ruth belted the last three homers of his epic career.

The Sultan of Swat

When Babe Ruth left baseball, the New York Yankees retired his famous Number 3 forever. He had become a legend, and no one else could ever take the great Bambino's place.

Babe Ruth grew up in St. Mary's Industrial School in Baltimore. Taught how to handle a needle, he was supposed to be a tailor, but Brother Gilbert suspected otherwise. Apparently, young Ruth was a rather good hand at pitching a baseball.

In 1914, he was signed by the minor-league Baltimore Orioles. Soon, he was picked up by the Boston Red Sox for $2,500.

In a few seasons, it became clear that Babe Ruth was the best lefthander in the American League. He helped pitch the Red Sox to three World's Championships, chalking up a brilliant pitching record of 29⅔ consecutive scoreless World Series innings. That mark stood for almost half a century.

But his dazzling record as a pitcher was soon eclipsed by his spectacular slugging. In 1918, he tied for home-run honors in the league with 11 circuit-drives. In 1919, the Babe's great war club clouted out a new record of 29—and baseball had a new hero. Then Colonel Ruppert bought him for New York, and the Yankees converted him to a full-time outfielder, so they could make full use of his hitting power.

Ruth knocked down record after record, each time setting up new ones only he could equal. During his 22 years in the major leagues, the socking Sultan of Swat hit 729 home runs, 15 of them in World Series play.

Opposing pitchers were so afraid of Ruth that they walked him 2,056 times. In the 1923 season alone, Ruth received 170 bases on balls, an average of over one per game.

In all, the Babe set up some 50 records. In the 1926 World Series, he socked three home runs in one game. In the 1928 World Series, he did it again. No one else has accomplished the feat of hitting three round-trippers in a single Series game. Ruth's batting average of .625 for that 1928 Series is still the top mark for championship play.

Babe Ruth gave baseball dozens of new records; but more importantly, Babe gave the game the warmth and color of his own personality. For the great Sultan of Swat—one might say single-handed—launched big-time baseball into a new era of glory.

Guilt by Association

The Black Sox Scandal of 1919—in which eight Chicago White Sox players conspired to fix the World Series—was an emotional trauma for the whole country. It violated the supposed purity of baseball, which most Americans viewed as a symbol of the national dedication to fair play.

In 1920, an overwrought young citizen of Joliet, Illinois, walked up to Buck Herzog, accused him of being "one of those crooked Chicago players," and slashed him with a knife.

The unfortunate Herzog was, indeed, a Chicago player, but he was a Cub.

Fit to Be Tied

The longest major league game that was ever played ended in a tie. On May 1, 1920, Brooklyn tackled Boston, and after 26 innings the umpire was forced to call it a no-decision bout. The shades of night fell on a hushed and awe-struck audience who watched Leon Cadore and Joe Oeschger pitch what amounted to almost three full games without relief.

Brooklyn scored in the fifth. Ernie Krueger walked, went to second on an infield out by Cadore, and raced to the plate on Ivy Olson's single.

Boston knotted the count in the sixth. With one out, Walton Cruise banged out a triple. Then Walter Holke flied to Zack Wheat. Wheat's wing was the talk of the league, and Cruise wisely hung onto third. Two down and Tony Boeckel up. Tony didn't fail! The third-baseman rapped out a single and Cruise scored.

From then on there were more goose eggs in the score than you could find in a hennery. For 17 long innings, both hurlers pitched shutout ball. It was one of the greatest artistic exhibitions in baseball history.

Too Many Two's

Only one player has ever died as a result of an injury sustained in a big-league game. On August 16, 1920, Cleveland shortstop

Ray Chapman was struck in the head by a fastball delivered by submarine pitcher Carl Mays. He died within hours.

Numerologists may be able to explain the strange box score Chapman left behind him on the day of his death, but it's a mystery to everyone in baseball. That day, Chapman batted in the number two slot in the Indian batting order. Before stepping to the plate for the final time, he had made two hits, both two-baggers. He had scored two runs, and had stolen two bases. In the field, he made two putouts, two assists, and two errors. And Chapman was even struck by two pitches, the second being the last pitch he ever saw.

Please, Guys, I'd Rather Do It Myself

It happened in a World Series. The date was October 10, 1920.

In the top half of the fifth, Pete Kilduff singled for Brooklyn. Otto Miller followed suit, Kilduff pulling up at second. No outs, two on. And though Clarence Mitchell, the Dodger pitcher, was now at bat, the top of the batting order was to follow.

Mitchell was determined to disprove the notion that hurlers can't hit. On the very first pitch, he slammed a screaming drive that was labeled "two-bagger." Seeing the ball streaking for the exits, the two baserunners dug in their spikes and made tracks down the basepaths.

But out of nowhere, Bill Wambsganss leaped into the air and stabbed the ball. In a flash, Wambsy stepped on second, doubling up Kilduff. Miller, who was pounding down to the keystone, put on the brakes and started back toward first. Bill gave hot pursuit. The chase ended halfway to first, Wambsy tagging Miller out.

The Cleveland second-sacker is the only man in World Series history who ever made an unassisted triple play.

ROGERS HORNSBY was a rather maniacal sort who, because he'd "eat, drink, and sleep" baseball, had little time for anything else. His only known amusements were race-horses and women, probably in that order. He neither drank nor smoked, and refused to go to the movies or to read anything in smaller type than a newspaper headline—he wanted to preserve his batting eye for when it counted.

One can hardly quarrel with the results. Between 1921 and 1925, the Rajah hit .397, .401, .384, .424, and .403—an average of .402! His lifetime mark of .358 is second only to that of Ty Cobb.

ON SEPTEMBER 4 and 5, 1921, Cleveland right-fielder Elmer Smith displayed something extra in the extra-base line. In seven consecutive times at bat, Smith drove out seven extra-baggers—four home runs and three doubles.

Elmer got himself a baseball record.

WAS THERE ever an odder hitter than Harry Heilmann? Four times during the 1920's he won the American League batting title, but only in the odd-numbered years—1921, 1923, 1925, and 1927. His averages for those seasons were .394, .403, .393, and .398. Not bad!

But Harry was no piker in the even-numbered years, either. His mark in 1922 was .356; in 1924, .346; and in 1926, .367.

IN A CAREER stretching over 21 years, Walter Johnson was never put out of a game by an umpire. What control!

A Fan's-Eye View

Chicago White Sox outfielder Ping Bodie was one of baseball's more colorful players in the 1910's. After a nine-year career in the majors, Ping decided to try his hand at umpiring, and landed a job with a small West Coast league.

One particular afternoon, the fans were riding Ping hard, and the oldtimer was getting a bit hot under his blue collar. Finally, he halted the game, walked over to the grandstand, and climbed up to a top-row seat.

The stunned players gathered in front of the stands and looked up at the ump in bewilderment. "What's going on?" one called out.

"If the fans can see 'em better from up here than I can down on the field," shouted Bodie, "then here is where I'll call 'em. Play ball!"

ONE OF BASEBALL'S best-known pitching exploits is Christy Mathewson's performance in the 1905 World Series against the Philadelphia's A's—three starts, three shutouts. But how many people know that in the 1921 Series, Waite Hoyt of the Yankees pitched every bit as well?

Hoyt won his first start against the Giants 3-0, and his second 3-1. He lost the final game of the Series to Art Nehf, 1-0. This may not seem to match up against Matty's three whitewashes, but only some sloppy work in the field by his Yankee mates deprived Hoyt of three shutouts. Both of the runs scored on him by the Giants were unearned.

The Ruth Tamer

Hub Pruett, a fair-to-middling pitcher, was one man who had the great Babe's number. Pruett was just a green kid hurling his first big-league season for the Browns when he faced the slugging Bambino for the first time. Though the Sultan of Swat was at the height of his terrific career, rookie Pruett struck out the great Babe.

And that first meeting established a pattern.

Pruett did it again and again. And still again. Time after time, the fence-busting slugger stood helpless against the astonishing lefty. In the first 23 times Hub Pruett faced Ruth, he fanned him 19 times. That was a performance no other pitcher was ever able to approach.

It's Never Too Late

Dazzy Vance won 197 games in his sparkling career, and is a member of the Hall of Fame. Yet he didn't win his first big-league game until he was 31 years old.

In 1915, Vance pitched a few games for the Pirates and the Yankees, posting a combined record of 0-4. A chronically sore arm forced him back to the minors, where he labored with little success until 1918, when the Yanks again took a look at him.

After two games, it was clear to the New York manager that Dazzy Vance just couldn't throw the ball with any velocity. He was duly returned to oblivion.

Over the next two and a half years, Vance went to scads of doctors and tried all sorts of wonder cures, but nothing did the trick until 1921, when he found that the formula for success was to pitch with more rest between starts.

Brooklyn bought him from Memphis after the 1921 season, and the rest is history. In his first four years with the Robins, as they were then called, Daz won 18, 18, 28, and 22. What with his late start, he didn't hang up his spikes until he was 44.

A Baseball Game or a Track Meet?

It happened on August 25, 1922. The tallies came in so thick and fast no one knew who succumbed more quickly, the pitchers or the scorekeepers.

In the wild-scoring melee, the Cubs came out on the long end of a 26-23 count.

It will surprise practically no one to learn that another all-

time record was set during the same nine innings. The Phillies slapped out 26 safeties and the Cubs 25, a total of 51 raps in one slap-happy game.

Goose-Egg Shampoo

When Walter Johnson raised the curtain on a season, he usually lowered the boom on the opposition. The noblest Senator of them all pitched the Washington team to shutout victories in seven opening-day games.

Strangely enough, the Big Train was particularly partial to the Athletics. He whitewashed the Philadelphians five times.

Fancy Fielding at First

Hal Chase is said to have used his shoe to catch a throw from his shortstop, but some say there has never been a better-fielding first-baseman than Wes Parker of the Dodgers. Still, it's hard to believe that either Chase or Parker had the agility and speed of foot possessed by the great George Sisler of the St. Louis Browns.

Sisler was the only first-bagger to start a double play on a suicide squeeze, the play in which the runner on third runs for home with the pitch, expecting the batter to bunt. It's generally held that on this play it is impossible to get the runner at home if the batter lays down any kind of bunt in fair territory. But on one occasion Sisler ran in, picked up the ball, and in one motion tagged the runner going to first and threw the ball home to nab the runner coming in from third!

Perhaps the most amazing of all Sisler's feats occurred one day against the Yanks. An opposing batter hit a grounder wide of first base which Sisler fielded in routine fashion and lobbed underhand to first, where the pitcher would arrive to meet the toss.

Only this time the pitcher must have been daydreaming, for he never left the mound. When Sisler realized that he had thrown the ball to a vacant base, he darted over to first and *caught his own throw*, in time to beat the Yankee runner!

FOR PITCHING CONTROL, it would be hard to top the feat of Stanley Coveleski, ace of the Cleveland mound staff from 1916 to 1924. In one game, Coveleski labored seven innings without throwing a single errant pitch. Every toss that wasn't hit came over the plate for a strike. Needless to note, Stanley wound up in the Hall of Fame.

ON SEPTEMBER 16, 1924, first-baseman Jim Bottomley of the St. Louis Cardinals set a major-league mark by driving in a dozen tallies in a single game.

Here's that Jim-dandy record:

1st inning:	Jim singled;	drove in 2 runs.
2nd inning:	Jim doubled;	drove in 1 run.
4th inning:	Jim homered;	drove in 4 runs.
6th inning:	Jim homered;	drove in 2 runs.
7th inning:	Jim singled;	drove in 2 runs.
9th inning:	Jim singled;	drove in 1 run.

Bottomley's feat that afternoon also put him in a tie for the major-league record of six hits by a batter in a nine-inning game.

The Pot and the Kettle

Pitcher Adolfo Luque and the Cincinnati Reds could not agree on salary terms for the upcoming season. After much futile bargaining, the Cincinnati owner wrote Luque that if he did not sign, Commissioner Landis would place Luque on a major-league blacklist.

Luque was enraged at this threat. Not trusting his hot temper, he enlisted the aid of fellow Cuban Pepe Conte in his salary negotiations. In the following letter to the Reds' owner, Conte skillfully conveyed Luque's feelings:

"I read your letter to him [Luque], and as he is the most illiterated man on captivity he raised cain and started to say at the top of his voice that you and Landis could go plump to ———. Of course, this is mere empty words pronounced by a man that has no education and that outside of his ability to pitch is a most perfect jack-ass."

The Keystone Rajah

"Get closer to the plate! Choke up on the bat! How do you expect to learn to hit that way?" Miller Huggins, manager of the 1915 Cardinals, was understandably exasperated.

The new infielder, just up from the Denison Club of the Western Association, stubbornly shook his head. He kept his stance at the extreme outside corner of the batter's box. He kept his hands together at the end of the handle.

Miller Huggins never did make him change his batting style. "Oh, well," the manager sighed philosophically, "what kind of a player can you expect to get for $400?"

Certainly not a league-leading batter. But *that's what Huggins got!* In fact, the Cards had obtained a slugger who was destined to lead the National League seven times, six of them in succession. Yes sir! Huggins had bought a .400 hitter for $400. Later, the Cardinals were to add a few zeros to that figure. In a few years, Hornsby was drawing down $40,000 a season.

Only three men in baseball history have ever hit .400 for three seasons: 1890's star Jesse Burkett, the immortal Cobb, and Hornsby. And the Rajah came within three points of reaching this mark a fourth time.

Hornsby holds the modern record for the highest batting average ever compiled during any one season. In 1924, the Rajah hit a resounding .424.

Although chiefly renowned today as a hitter, Rogers was a ball of fire who inspired his team to a pitch of fighting spirit. It was manager Hornsby who led the Cardinals to their first pennant and to a victory over the Yankees in the World Series. But Hornsby's hitting was so spectacular that all his other achievements have more or less paled. For with a lifetime average of .358, the Rajah was the greatest batsman the National League has ever seen.

Lady Luck Smiles on Old Barney

"Washington: first in war, first in peace—and last in the American League." That was the popular quip about the Senators in the first decade of the century.

Even Walter Johnson, the great speedball artist, couldn't change his team's losing habits. It began to look as though the greatest hurler of them all might never get a chance to pitch a World Series.

Fortunately, Johnson was durable as well as artful. In 1924, the great righthander still had enough stuff to win 23 and lose only seven. Seventeen years after he had started his major-league career, Old Barney led the league in pitching. By now, the Senators had amassed enough batting power to crash through to their first pennant.

To Johnson went the honor of pitching the opener against the Giants. It was an extra-inning heartbreaker. The Giants won in the twelfth.

In the fifth game, Johnson lost again. But Tom Zachary and George Mogridge won three games to keep the Senators in the race.

On October 10, 1924, in the seventh and deciding game, Bucky Harris put Johnson in as a relief pitcher in the ninth inning.

It was a lulu of a battle. When the ninth inning ended, the score was knotted at three runs apiece. Neither team scored in the tenth. Neither team scored in the eleventh. In the last of the twelfth with one out, Muddy Ruel, Washington backstop, caught one on the handle of his bat and popped a puny foul. Hank

Gowdy, the Giant catcher, whipped off his mask and started after it. But here Fate took a hand. Gowdy didn't notice that his mask had rolled in front of him. His eyes turned skyward, he jammed a foot plunk into the mask and fell to earth. So did the ball.

That was the big break. Ruel made good his reprieve and lashed out a two-bagger. Johnson reached first on an error. Then Earl McNeely drove a hard grounder down to Freddy Lindstrom at third. It looked like a double play, but the ball struck a pebble a yard in front of Lindstrom, and bounded over the third-base-man's head into left field. Ruel crossed the plate with the winning run.

No one begrudged Johnson his victory. Even Jack Bentley, the losing Giant pitcher, was cheerful about it. "I guess the good Lord couldn't stand seeing Walter Johnson lose again," he said. So on two flukes in the twelfth inning, Walter Johnson fulfilled his life-long dream of winning a World Series game!

IN A GAME against the Yankees in 1925, Philadelphia third-baseman Jimmy Dykes came up against Garland Braxton four times and made four base hits, each on the first pitch. By the time he strode to the plate for his fifth turn, Herb Pennock had replaced starter Braxton.

Yank backstop Benny Bengough gave Pennock the sign to throw one under Dykes' chin, but Pennock kept shaking it off. At last Bengough screamed out, "For Pete's sake, he's got four hits already!"

Pennock simply grinned and said, "Let's see if he can get another."

The first pitch came in over the plate, and Dykes laced it out for his fifth hit.

Anything for a Laugh

When the Chicago Cubs opened spring training in 1925, the big talk was of two new faces. Veteran infielders Rabbit Maranville and Charlie Grimm had arrived from Pittsburgh where they had nearly driven manager Bill McKechnie crazy with their high-jinks.

Mindful of their reputation for making news, a photographer joined the two clowns out on the golf course at Catalina Island, where the Cubs trained in the spring. At the photog's request, first-baseman Grimm posed flat on his back with a golf tee between his teeth; Rabbit stood above him, clutching a driver in mock readiness.

The shot was set. "Okay, hold it!" the shutterbug yelled, whereupon Rabbit took a mighty cut and knocked the ball clean off the tee in Charlie's mouth, and over the photographer's head. The usually jovial Grimm was grim indeed when he arose, for though Rabbit had hit many a baseball in his day, he'd not played more than a few rounds of golf in his life.

So Take That!

There is no argument as to who was baseball's best hitter—the answer must be Ty Cobb. However, some observers feel that he didn't hit the long ball, and consequently was less valuable to the Tiger team than, say, Babe Ruth was to the Yanks.

But Cobb was a powerful man in his own right, and had he chosen to, he could have hit many more home runs than the 118 he poled during his 24-year career. To prove that he was a slashing-type hitter by choice, on May 5, 1925, he announced that he would go for the fences for a couple of days. That same afternoon, he hit three homers. The next day, he walloped two more.

Having made his point, he went back to place-hitting and finished the season with an average of .378. And the Georgia Peach was then 38 years old!

The Babe Strikes Back

The great Babe was as helpless as an infant in the first three games of the 1926 World Series. The St. Louis mound staff had kept the Bambino well in check, allowing him only two measly hits in all three games.

But in the fourth contest, on October 6, 1926, the sleeping Babe awoke and started kicking with a vengeance. In the first frame, the Redbird twirler, Flint Rhem, had whiffed Earle Combs and Mark Koenig on seven pitched balls. When Ruth, No. 3 in the Yankee batting order, stepped to the plate, the fans began to hoot, "Put in a pinch-hitter!"

For his first offering, the confident Rhem served up a fast-breaking curve. Wham! By twisting his head quickly, Rhem could see a little white speck soaring high over the right-field fence. The crowd was stunned into a silence so complete you could have heard a pin drop. But not the ball. That landed outside the park on Grand Avenue, some 400 feet from home plate.

There were two out again in the third frame when the Babe came up to bat. This time Rhem tried a slow floater. The change of pace didn't change his luck. The eyes of a startled crowd of Card rooters watched the pellet follow its predecessor in a non-stop flight over the right-field stockade.

In the fourth, Art Reinhart, who had been rushed in as relief for the badly shattered Rhem, handled Ruth with more respect. He was taking no chances. Four balls outside the plate were better than one over the fence. So Ruth got a walk.

But the cautious Reinhart couldn't afford such luxury in the sixth. Then, when the bulk that was Babe appeared in the batter's box, there were two men on. A pass would only mean that Reinhart would have to face Gehrig with the bases full—a noxious prospect for any pitcher. So Reinhart elected to pitch.

The count stood 3 and 2; the crowd waited tensely. Reinhart tried to uncoil a fast one over the inside corner. Somewhere in mid-flight, the horsehide collided with three pounds of seasoned ash and changed its direction of travel.

The ball took an express passage to the center-field seats, a mere 450 feet away—the mightiest wallop ever generated in the Missouri park. This was Babe's third homer of the day, and a World Series record.

This time, as the Babe ambled around the bases with his usual ponderous grace, the crowd, silent and resentful on his first two drives, climbed to its feet and cheered!

You just couldn't stay mad at the Babe.

Ol' Pete's Finest Hour

For sheer, concentrated diamond drama, little can match the seventh inning of the seventh game of the 1926 World Series. The Yankees, heavy favorites, were old hands at the classic. The underdog Cardinals, fresh from their first pennant, were eagerly battling to crown their season with the World's Championship. The amazing fact that the Series went into the final game tied at three games apiece was due in no small degree to the efforts of a used-up old Cardinal hurler named Grover Cleveland Alexander.

Ol' Pete, then 39 years old and a veteran of 16 years in the majors, was well past his prime. But he still had enough to muffle the murderous Yankee bats and win the second game of the Series handily. In the sixth game, too, just the day before, Alex had gone the full nine-inning route to defeat the Yankees a second time, and even up the Series.

Now, in the seventh and decisive game, on October 10, the Redbirds held on for dear life to a razor-thin 3-2 lead. The St. Louis hurler, Jess Haines, was working craftily and effectively despite a blister that was beginning to form on his middle finger. But in the seventh, Haines began to falter. He walked Earle Combs, the first Yankee to face him. On a sacrifice by Mark Koenig, Combs moved up to second, and the Babe came up. This was no time to trifle with the Bambino's ruthless bludgeon, so Jess handed him an intentional pass. Haines won a momentary reprieve when Bob Meusel's grounder forced Ruth at second. Two down.

But now Jess' finger was giving him real trouble. Four wide ones put Lou Gehrig on first, and the bases were full. And at the bat-pile, picking out his club, was eager, hard-hitting, young Tony Lazzeri.

From second base, manager Rogers Hornsby called time. He walked to the pitcher's box and inspected Haines' damaged digit. The blister had opened and was bleeding. The Rajah looked up and beckoned to the bullpen, where Flint Rhem and Art Reinhart were warming up. But the signal was not for either of them. A third man—a hunched, shambling figure—started toward the infield. Grover Cleveland Alexander shuffled in to keep a date with destiny.

The suspense of the moment made that slow walk in from the bullpen seem interminable. From the hushed silence of the stands, one might easily have taken it for the death march.

Why, many wondered, was it Alexander, and not Reinhart or Rhem, coming in toward the mound? After his nine-inning chore of the day before, Ol' Pete had no reasonable expectation that he would be called on again. In view of that, he had done some celebrating—perhaps a little too much celebrating—the night before. Was he rested enough—was he in condition to pitch?

Hornsby met him at the sideline. For a moment the manager looked into the old hurler's eyes. What he saw there reassured him. Hornsby said quietly, "Go to it. You can do it, Pete."

Alexander's first toss was a feeler. Lazzeri refused to bite. Ball one. Then came a low fast one. A called strike. One and one. Tony lashed at the next one.

The piercing crack was like a rifle report. Thirty-eight thousand fans jumped to their feet howling, as a mighty line drive whistled toward the left-field stands. The ball zoomed over the fence and the shouts rose to a deafening roar—and then suddenly died away. The drive was foul by a foot! The disappointed Yankee runners retreated to their bases.

Alex wound up again. Everything the aging arm had left went into the next pitch. Lazzeri took aim, swung venomously— and missed! Strike three!

For all practical purposes, that ended the ballgame. Alex set down the Yanks without much trouble in the eighth and ninth frames, and Herb Pennock of the New Yorkers returned the compliment. The 3-2 score stood, and the hysterical Cards carried the Series crown back to St. Louis.

BABE RUTH'S 60 home runs in 1927 accounted for a staggering 13.7 percent of all the four-baggers hit in the American League. Today, a player would have to hit 180 homers to achieve the same measure of domination. Singlehanded, the Bambino hit more home runs in 1927 than 12 of the other 15 teams in the major leagues!

Don't Bother Me, Kid

During the 1928 season, Dodger manager Wilbert Robinson decided that his rookie catcher, Al Lopez, was too green to call his own signals. So Uncle Robbie called them from the bench.

The arrangement worked well until one afternoon when the Bums locked horns with the Pirates. Trailing 2-1 in the ninth, the Bucs loaded the bases with no outs, and the next two batters were Lloyd Waner and his brother Paul. Two of the most formidable batters of their day, they were nicknamed "Little Poison" and "Big Poison."

Lopez looked over to the bench to get his signs. Robinson couldn't quite figure out how to handle the situation, so he tied his shoes, took a drink of water—in short, did anything he could to avoid looking toward the plate.

Finally, Lopez strolled over to the bench to get his instructions.

"What's the matter, Lopez?" Robinson snapped. "You never catch in the big leagues before?"

If This Is Salt Lake City, I Must Be an Outfielder

Lefty O'Doul was a terrible pitcher. In part-seasons during four years with the Yankees and Red Sox, he won the grand total of one game. In 1923, Lefty gave up 13 runs in one inning.

At the end of that season, Boston sold him to Salt Lake City of the Pacific Coast League. When O'Doul saw how the high altitude transformed fly balls into tape-measure homers, he decided that his pitching days were over.

"I am now an outfielder," Lefty told the manager.

"But you don't know how to play the outfield," the skipper replied.

"Well," said Lefty, "I'll learn."

And he did—so well, in fact, that he led the league in hitting with a .392 mark.

In 1928, O'Doul made his return to the big time with the New York Giants, and hit .319. The next year, with the Phillies, he played in every game, hit .398, and laced out 254 hits, a National League record. He finished his career in 1934 with a lifetime batting mark of .349. Only three men of baseball's modern era had a higher average.

O'Doul was not to play his final game of professional ball until 1956, 22 years after he had hung up his spikes in the majors. While managing Vancouver in the Coast League, one day O'Doul needed a pinch-hitter. He looked down his bench, saw nothing too promising, and sent himself up to bat. The 59-year-old O'Doul had not forgotten how to hit. He smacked a triple.

How Not to Bunt

Bunting is an essential part of any team's offense, but few sluggers like to sacrifice a chance to hit the ball out. Babe Herman was no exception. One afternoon, the Brooklyn star stepped to the plate with a man on first and nobody out. Dodger manager Wilbert Robinson called for the bunt. Babe chuckled, then muttered to the batboy, "If Robbie thinks I'm gonna bunt, he's crazy. Watch this!"

Herman purposely bunted the first two pitches foul, then drove the third high over the right-field wall. As Herman rounded the bases, Robinson shook his head and grunted, "I shoulda known the Babe can't bunt."

Other players have not been so fortunate in crossing the manager. Red Murray, an outfielder with the New York Giants in the 1910's, stepped to the plate in the ninth inning of a tie game with Pittsburgh. With a man on second and no out, manager John McGraw followed orthodox strategy and signaled Murray to lay one down the third-base line.

However, Pirate pitcher Howie Camnitz smelled the call and threw his pitch high and tight. But that was Murray's alley. He swung away and sent the ball over the left-field fence to win the game.

Red whistled his way around the bases and into the shower. But he changed his tune when McGraw found him in the clubhouse and fined him $100 for disregarding a sign.

No one more courteous and polite than Pie Traynor ever appeared on the diamond. Traynor was known throughout the league as a perfect gentleman. He never used profanity, no matter what the provocation.

One day, Pie was ejected from the field by Umpire Bill Klem. There was no apparent reason for this drastic move, and later the arbiter was queried by a reporter. When asked for the reason, Umpire Klem explained that Traynor wasn't feeling well.

"Whaddya mean he wasn't feeling well?" asked the reporter. "There was nothing wrong with him that I could see."

"Well," said Klem, "that's what he told me. He came up to

me like the perfect gentleman he is and said, 'Mr. Klem, I'm sick and tired of your stupid decisions.' "

But What Did His Daughter Say?

Joe Cronin was playing for a minor-league outfit in Kansas City when a Senator scout purchased his contract for $7,500. The scout returned to the capital with the shortstop under his wing, and headed straight for owner Clark Griffith's office. When they arrived, Griffith's daughter was just about to leave.

"Hey, Mildred," the scout bubbled, "I brought you a husband from Kansas City! Meet Joe Cronin."

Sure enough, Joe soon married the boss' daughter. He also became the best shortstop in baseball; and at age 26 he was appointed the Senators' manager.

But when it came to business, Mr. Griffith was not one to let his heart rule his head. When Boston offered him $250,000 plus a shortstop for Cronin's contract, Griffith readily agreed to the transaction. It is the only instance of a baseball owner peddling his own son-in-law.

ON SEPTEMBER 17, 1928, in the ninth inning of a game with the Cubs, the Braves sent Ray Boggs to the mound as a relief pitcher. Boggs promptly proceeded to hit three batters with pitched balls.

This record of unpremeditated assault remains unsurpassed in major-league chronicles.

UMPIRE BILL GUTHRIE sure knew how to handle a boy with a temper.

Once a player, in a white rage over a called strike, took his bat and flung it high in the air. Guthrie removed his mask and eyed the soaring bludgeon.

"Son," he said softly, "if that bat comes down, you're out of the game."

The Washington Express

For the most part, there wasn't anything tricky about Walter Johnson's delivery. He just threw a fastball. If that didn't work, he threw a faster one. That didn't give batters much comfort, but it did provide them with a ready-made alibi: "How can you hit 'em if you can't see 'em?"

In one game, Ray Chapman took two burning strikes from Johnson. Then he stepped out of the batter's box and started back for the dugout. "Wait a minute," called the umpire, "you've got another strike coming."

"Never mind," shrugged Chapman, "I don't want it."

That was Chapman's privilege, but Walter Johnson had no objections to giving batters their full allotment of three strikes. In his 21-year career, the Big Train dished out 3,508 strikeouts— a record that looks safe for all time. During that time Johnson led the league in K's for 12 years.

The great Washington righthander was never out to set records. His object was to win ballgames. That he did, chalking up 414 victories for a generally weak Washington club.

In one memorable game, it looked as though the Big Train was about to be derailed. The bases had suddenly filled with Red Sox on an error, a hit batter, and a base on balls—all charged to Johnson. To make things darker, none were out. Shortstop George McBride called time and walked in to give Johnson a few well-meant words of advice.

"Now, now, George," Johnson chided gently. "Suppose you go back and play shortstop, and let me do the pitching."

The Big Train then opened the throttle and fanned Tris Speaker, Harry Hooper, and Duffy Lewis on nine straight pitches!

Johnson was the greatest goose-egg merchant the game has ever known. Sir Walter hung up a lifetime record of 113 shutout games.

When he was really hot, opposing players would touch their spikes on the plate for luck. That was the best they could do. They couldn't touch it to score. For a period of over a month— from April 10 to May 14, 1913—no one pushed across a single run against Johnson! When the Browns finally managed to drive a tally across the plate in the fourth inning of a lopsided game on May 14, they ended Johnson's staggering streak of 56 scoreless innings! No hurler was able to match this magnificent performance for 55 years.

The Clown Prince of Baseball

After a short career in the majors, former Senator Al Schacht toured the minor leagues with a one-man clowning act. One day a friend who was managing a bush team in Olean, New York, invited Al up to do a show. Attendance that year had been terrible, and he offered the clown $150 for the stint, plus an extra $100 in the unlikely event that Schacht could draw 2,500 fans.

The Clown Prince of Baseball performed in Olean before a surprisingly large crowd, dressed, and went to the ticket office to pick up his pay. The manager was pleased and offered Schacht a check for $150.

Al asked for the attendance figure, and when he was informed that it was 2,492, a season high, he told the manager to hold the check. Then the clown went out and bought eight bleacher seats for 50¢ each, bringing the total gate to exactly 2,500.

Schacht then returned to the ticket office and demanded the extra $100. His friend had no choice but to fork over the full amount.

Fans who like to watch the ball riding for the fences got their money's worth in a game between the Pittsburghers and the Phillies on July 10, 1929.

Every inning of that unique contest was enlivened by one home run—no more, no less.

It's Not Whether You Win...

In baseball, the front office and the dugout don't usually mix. Not that it hasn't been tried.

In 1929, the manager's post on the Boston Braves fell vacant. Judge Emil Fuchs, pompous owner and chairman of the board, decided to economize by taking over the field direction of the team himself. The way he saw it, the manager's job was a luxury that could be dispensed with. The Judge felt he could handle it very nicely by keeping some of the older heads around him as an advisory board.

Once the Braves had the bases loaded and were badly in need of a run. Fuchs called a hasty conference of his brain-trust. "It's a good time for a squeeze play," said the spokesman.

The good Judge was outraged. "I won't hear of it!" he roared. "I want to win as much as any of you—but either we win honorably or not at all!"

THERE WERE no flies on Earl Clark on May 10, 1929—but many a fly in his glove.

All that afternoon, the Boston outfielder kept plucking balls out of the ozone. When the day's activities were over, Earl found himself credited with an even dozen putouts. For an outfielder that's one for the books.

Clark even found time to throw a runner out on the basepaths. Things were just going his way that afternoon.

Just Another Ballgame

In the late '20s, the Dodgers and the Pirates were locked in a close game at Pittsburgh's Forbes Field. Trailing 2-1 in the ninth, the Bucs put two men aboard with two out. But the rally seemed to die as Pie Traynor drove a liner toward Babe Herman in the outfield which appeared to be a sure out. But the Babe charged, tripped, and fell flat on his face. As the ball rolled to the fence, the winning runs crossed the plate.

The Dodgers trudged to the clubhouse in defeat. But the compassionate Dodger manager, Wilbert Robinson, put his arm around Herman.

"What happened, Babe?" he asked solicitously.

"When?" Babe replied.

NOT FOR NOTHING did they cáll John McGraw "Little Napoleon." He was an absolute tyrant in the dugout, treating his ballplayers like unruly children.

Rogers Hornsby once expatiated about McGraw's insistence upon keeping his men in line. "He'd warn players against becoming too buddy-buddy with sportswriters. One rookie was so scared that he'd rub McGraw the wrong way, that when a writer asked him 'Are you married?' the rookie answered, 'You'd better ask Mr. McGraw.'"

Mutual Admiration Society

Umpires, usually the targets of verbal abuse, occasionally get the opportunity to strike back. One afternoon in Chicago, umpire Red Ormsby was getting the business from the fans. A robust woman in a first-base box was giving him a particularly rough time. During a lull in the general barrage, the woman's voice could distinctly be heard to shout, "You blind bum! If you were my husband, I'd give you poison!"

With great dignity, the beleagured arbiter strolled toward the first-base box, removed his hat, and bowed reverently before his loud-mouthed heckler. Then, for the benefit of all the fans, he roared, "Madam, if you were my wife, I'd take it!"

The Pride of Flatbush

They called him the incredible Hoiman, the Dean of the Daffiness Boys. The Babe was a murderous performer with the bat. And in the field—that was murder, too!

Floyd Caves Herman started as a first-baseman, and while he could generally hang on to enough throws to keep the franchise, his own throws were wondrous to behold. "Whenever the opponents got two men on base and Babe got hold of the ball," wrote Kyle Crichton in *Collier's*, "the players in both dugouts dropped down behind the concrete and hid, fans in all parts of the field cowered in fright, and the groundskeepers hastily locked the gates to keep the ball in the park."

But Babe's bleacher-busting bat had to be kept in the lineup. Wilbert Robinson harked to the old proverb: "If at first you don't succeed—try the outfield."

So Uncle Robbie dispatched Herman to greener pastures. As an outfielder, Babe didn't change the error of his ways, but he did change the way of his errors.

No one could possibly have dreamed how many different ways there were of missing a fly ball. But Herman showed them. It was always a toss-up whether Herman would drop the ball— or the ball would drop Herman.

The Babe always bitterly denied the story that he had once been hit on the head by a pop fly. "Why," he told a newspaper man, "if a ball ever hit me on the head, I'd just hang up my glove and quit baseball. You can write that."

"How about your shoulder?" pursued the scribe. "Would that still go if a ball dropped on your shoulder?"

"Oh, no!" Herman answered hastily. "The shoulder don't count. Only the head!"

Unquestionably, the most famous of Herman's incredible exploits with the Flatbush Flock was the time he doubled into a double play. Actually!

In a game with the Braves in 1926, the bases were chock-full of Dodgers. Hank De Berry was parked on third, Dazzy Vance was camping on second, and Chick Fewster was on first. All were looking toward the plate awaiting the go signal from the clattering club of Herman. It came—a long high drive that bounced off the right-field wall. De Berry raced home for a score. Vance and Fewster took off from second and first. The Babe himself broke from the barrier like Man O' War in his friskier days.

Vance rounded third, and then had a change of heart. He reversed his field and started back for the bag. Fewster was pounding down from second and Herman, his head down and still charging, crossed the keystone sack and headed toward third. They all hit the dirt, head first. In a swirling cloud of dust, all three met noggin to noggin at third base!

When in due course the ball arrived, all that remained was for the third-sacker to lay the tag on the three dormant Dodgers. Umpire Quigley ruled that Vance held the lease on third base and so he couldn't be evicted, but that Herman and Fewster were indubitably, incontrovertibly, and incorrigibly O-U-T!

A wide-eyed Flatbush rookie, watching the proceedings with amazement, turned to manager Robbie. "Mr. Robinson," he gasped, "what kind of baseball is that?"

"Leave them be!" snapped Uncle Wilbert. "That's the first time they've been together all season!"

It was an unknown cabdriver who made the classic remark about the Daffiness Boys. Seated in his hack, parked outside Ebbets Field, the cabbie spoke to an early-leaving spectator. "How're our bums doing?" he asked.

"Swell," assured the fan. "The Dodgers are ahead, and we got three men on base."

"You don't say," replied the deadpan driver. "Which base?"

Babe Herman was one of the few ballplayers capable of stealing second with the bases full. Yet he always felt he was badly used by the press. Once, more in sorrow than in anger, he sounded off to a columnist.

"Why," he complained, "why do you guys always harp on me? Just because you gotta have something to write about every day in the papers, why do you always make me out like a clown? Fun's fun and all that, but I'm a family man, and showing me up like a screwball don't help me in the game, and I gotta make a living same as you guys."

By this time, the writer was feeling more than a little apologetic. Maybe, after all, they had been giving poor Babe a raw deal. As the repentant newsman shifted uneasily from foot to foot, Herman reached into his vest pocket, hauled out the stub of a cigar, and put it in his mouth.

"Here, I'll give you a light," said the writer, reaching into his pocket.

"Don't bother," said Herman, puffing a cloud of smoke as he walked away, "It's lit already."

One Base Is Better Than Four

On April 30, 1944, opposing pitchers rolled out the red carpet for Giant slugger Mel Ott. They gave him five bases on balls. But the quintet of free passes was nothing new to Mel. He had been the recipient of five walks on three previous occasions.

The first time he received such treatment was on the next-to-last day of the 1929 season. In the first game of a doubleheader against the Phillies, Ott smacked his 42nd homer of the year. This put him one up on Phils' star Chuck Klein for the circuit-blow crown. But Klein came back in that same game with two homers of his own to regain the lead.

In the second game of the doubleheader, Ott was given an

intentional pass each time he came to the plate—in the first, third, fourth, and sixth innings. But when Mel came to bat in the eighth, the bags were full of Giants. The Phils' pitcher looked to the dugout for instructions. The manager did not hesitate a moment—though his team was still in a position to win the game, he motioned to put Ott on. The pitcher proceeded to issue four straight balls, and Mel trotted to first as a run crossed the plate.

Ott thus won the distinction of becoming the only player besides Babe Ruth to receive an intentional pass with the bases loaded. But he lost the home-run title to Klein, 43-42.

And to Show You How It's Done...

Brooklyn manager Wilbert Robinson was fed up with the shoddy play of his 1920's Dodgers. To keep the Daffiness Boys on their toes, he formed the "Bonehead Club." Each time some player pulled a bonehead play, he'd have to pay a fine to the Club.

Uncle Robbie, however, was the first to fill the coffers of his elite society. One day, he walked up to home plate prior to the start of the game, and instead of submitting a lineup card to the umpire, he handed the ump a laundry slip.

Going Out in a Blaze of Glory

The fans could scarcely believe their ears when the starting battery for the Athletics was announced. In the Philadelphia dugout, the players were staring at each other in dismay. Across the field, on the Cubs' bench, the jubilation was unrestrained. Old Howard Ehmke was going to start the 1929 Series opener? Someone must be crazy—and that someone could only be Connie Mack!

It was true that Ehmke had once been a stellar moundsman, but everyone knew he was through. That season he had pitched only two complete games for the A's. When the club took its final Western swing, Ehmke hadn't even been taken along. Everybody knew Ehmke was a has-been—but here he was, about to start the all-important first game of the Series!

Connie Mack had sent Howard Ehmke to scout the Cubs,

who had already clinched the National League flag. If Ehmke felt that his old soupbone could go the route, Mack had promised to start him. Maybe it was a sentimental promise. But Mack was as good as his word.

Few would have been surprised to see the oldtimer blasted out of the box in the first inning that October 8, 1929. But as the afternoon wore on, Ehmke proved that his old craft was still there. His long rest and the rays of a warm autumn sun combined to loosen up and restore zip to the old muscles.

Inning after inning, the baffled Cubs went down before the old master's sleight of hand. They got hits, yes—eight of them. But in the pinch, old Howard still had what it takes. He fanned the great Rogers Hornsby twice. Slugging champ Hack Wilson also took the three-strike treatment on two trips to the plate.

Going into the ninth, Ehmke had fanned 12 men, tying the World Series record set in 1906 by Big Ed Walsh. The Cubs had yet to score.

But in the ninth, it began to look as though the old firehorse had shot his bolt. With the A's guarding a 3-0 lead, the Cubs began to reach Ehmke. The rescue squad began to warm up in the A's bullpen. The Cubs had shoved a run across the plate. With two out and the tying runs on base, a Cub pinch-hitter came to bat.

Could old Howard bear down just once more? Did he have enough reserve to come through in the pinch? The washed-out vet summoned all the experience of his years, and the last ounce of energy left in his quivering frame.

In spite of themselves, the Chicago fans couldn't help cheering as the pinch-hitter went down swinging for the 13th strikeout of the game—a World Series record that stood for more than 20 years!

Connie Mack had gambled on getting one more good performance out of the fading Howard Ehmke, and a great pitcher hurled an immortal game—the last he ever won.

Back from the Brink

The score was so one-sided it was practically no contest. A few prudent fans left the park early to avoid the rush. But the prudent missed the most astounding rally in World Series history.

This was October 12, 1929. Coming up to the last half of the seventh, it looked as though the Cubs had the game on ice. They were atop an 8-0 score. Their pitching ace, Charlie Root, had been practically inaccessible.

Came the seventh, the first man up for the A's, Al Simmons, poled out a home run. That didn't worry the Cubs much. After all, it was only one run.

But then a staccato of singles rattled off the bats of Jimmy Foxx, Bing Miller, Jimmy Dykes, and Joe Boley. Two more runs crossed the plate and the mastodonic lead of eight was whittled down to a merely colossal five.

When pinch-hitter George Burns popped to the infield, it looked as if Charlie Root was once more in control. But Max Bishop promptly singled, driving still another run across. This was enough for Manager Joe McCarthy, and he sent an S.O.S. to the bullpen. Veteran Art Nehf came in to replace Root. With the score 8-4, the brooding Philly crowd was beginning to come to life; to the unprejudiced, however, the four-run lead seemed as solid as concrete.

Mule Haas brought the stands to their feet with a whistling line drive to deep center. And then came the big break. Hack Wilson lost the ball in the glaring sun. Before he recovered the ball, Haas had rounded the bags, sending in two runs ahead of him. That made the score 8-7, but now the bases were clear.

They didn't stay that way for long. The shaken Nehf passed Mickey Cochrane. That washed him up. McCarthy sent in Sheriff Blake to stem the tide.

Now Al Simmons came to bat for the second time. He celebrated this fact with a solid single. Jimmy Foxx followed with another smash that propelled Cochrane across with the tying run. Sheriff Blake went off to write his memoirs.

When Pat Malone, the fourth Cub pitcher, took his place on the rubber, there was Simmons perched on third and Foxx dancing off first. To keep the proceedings from getting into a rut, Malone hit Bing Miller with a pitched ball, thus filling the bases.

And when Jimmy Dykes punched out a vicious double, scoring Simmons and Foxx, all pandemonium broke loose.

When quiet was restored, Malone struck out Boley and Burns to wind up the massacre.

So ended the biggest inning in World Series history. Evidently, in baseball, a game isn't over—well, till it's over!

Eddie Collins' Quarter-Century

Major-league baseball has been a going institution for almost a century, since the founding of the National League in 1876. And second-baseman Eddie Collins played in the big time for a quarter of that span—the longest major-league career of any player. (Cap Anson played professional ball for 27 years, but five of those years came prior to 1876.)

Collins began with the Athletics in 1906, and stayed with the Mackmen until 1914. From 1915 to 1926, he played for the White Sox. In 1927, he returned to the Philadelphia fold, and remained with the A's until he turned in his spikes in 1930.

Throughout his long career, Collins was one of baseball's stellar attractions. Many authorities count Eddie as the best second-sacker that ever wore a uniform. He was a most reliable batsman, carving out a career average of .333. Fast and clever on the paths, Eddie piled up a lifetime total of 744 stolen bases.

USUALLY, MORE BUSINESS is done on first base than on any area of the diamond. But on April 27, 1930, first-baseman Bud Clancy of the Chisox played a full nine-inning game against the St. Louis

Browns without even getting his hands on the ball. Not one of the 27 putouts came Bud's way, nor did he even make an assist.

Clancy's record for a first-baseman's laziest day in baseball has since been equaled, but it's safe to say that it will never be bettered.

THE PHILADELPHIA PHILLIES of 1930 could really hit the ball. That year, the Phils had eight-players with averages of .313 or better. Still they finished last, forty games off the mark.

Impossible? Not when your pitchers are giving up 7.7 runs a game—the worst pitching performance by any team in the history of baseball.

Danger: Man on Diet

During the 1920's and 1930's, the rotund figure of Fat Fothergill was a well-known sight in American League ballparks. Over a span of 12 years, Fatty wielded the bat for a .326 career average, but he could wield the knife and fork with equal dexterity. One day, Detroit manager George Moriarty, after witnessing Fat devour five steaks, let the slow-footed outfielder have it hard.

"That's it, Fat," he roared across the table, "Get yourself down to 200 pounds or you're out of a job!"

Faced with the prospect of minor-league cuisine, the dismayed Fothergill went on a crash diet. He managed to shed a few pounds, but his nerves were fraying fast.

One afternoon, after an unsympathetic umpire called Fat out on strikes, the corpulent Tiger cracked. Flinging his bat down in a rage, he lunged at the surprised arbiter and bit him on the arm.

Needless to say, Fat was given an immediate thumb. But he was smiling broadly as he returned to the dugout.

"I don't mind," he laughed contentedly. "That's the first bite of meat I've had in weeks!"

IN HIS SPRIGHTLIER DAYS, the great Babe Ruth was a tough nut for any manager to crack. Completely aware of how much he

107

meant to his team, Ruth used to defy all training rules and his manager as well.

Finally, skipper Miller Huggins couldn't stand it any longer, and advised a press conference that he was really going to clamp down on the Bambino. "I'll talk to him," said Huggins. "I'll talk to him, all right."

A short while later, the bulky Bambino came strutting along with a big, black cigar in his mouth. One of the newsmen got ahold of Huggins and said, "There's the Babe coming along now. Let's see you talk to him."

"You bet," snapped Huggins. Then as the towering Ruth approached, the little manager took one look at that overpowering figure and piped, "Hiya, Babe!"

Miller Huggins had talked to him, all right!

Touching Four Bases

There was the time Casey Stengel doffed his cap to the cheers of the crowd and a sparrow flew out of his hair and circled the field.

There was the time Tony Cuccinello loped into third base standing up and was put out. He didn't attempt a slide, he explained to his manager, because he was afraid he might bust the cigars in his pocket.

There was the time one of the Washington Senators sent a screaming drive into the left-field stands. After the umpire had run down the left-field line and called the ball fair, he noticed that a woman was being carried from the pavilion. The arbiter asked coach Nick Altrock whether the woman had been hit. "No!" answered Nick so all the fans could hear. "You called that one right and she passed out in shock!"

And there was the time that Art Shires responded to the boos of the bleachers by turning to the crowd and shouting, "Good! That's all right. Go ahead. I get excited, too, when I see a great ballplayer!"

Pardon My Blooper

As great a ballplayer as Lou Gehrig was, he never seized the public's fancy in the way Babe Ruth did. While the Babe made hundreds of thousands of dollars from public appearances, exhibitions, and endorsements, Larrupin' Lou hardly made a cent. He simply lacked Ruth's charisma—but then again, didn't everyone?

On one of the few occasions that Gehrig picked up an endorsement, he fumbled it. Once, he was signed to go on radio to plug a breakfast cereal called Huskies.

"To what do you owe your strength and condition?" the announcer asked.

"Wheaties," Gehrig replied.

The mortified Gehrig refused to accept any money for the commercial, but the company insisted. Huskies had gained more publicity from Gehrig's boner than the cereal could ever have achieved if the commercial had gone smoothly.

GEORGE EARNSHAW, who in his day pitched a lot of fine ball for the Athletics, once faced the Yanks when their famed "Murderers' Row" was in a particularly homicidal mood. Lou Gehrig in his first two times at bat had found two of Earnshaw's offerings to his liking, and deposited them both in the right-field stands.

After Larrupin' Lou's second circuit-drive, the disgusted Connie Mack yanked Earnshaw and sent in Popeye Mahaffey to pitch. Earnshaw sat glumly on the bench next to Mack and watched the relief pitcher retire the Yanks.

Next time Gehrig stepped to the plate, Mack turned to the dejected righthander and said, "Keep an eye on this. I want you to see what can be done with this Gehrig guy if you just pitch him right."

Mahaffey wound up and delivered. There was a sharp crack and the anguished Athletics watched the ball sailing high over the left-field fence for another Gehrig homer.

After a moment's silence, Earnshaw spoke. "Yes, I see what you mean, Mr. Mack," he said. "Mahaffey sure made Gehrig hit in a different direction."

What Might Have Been

On April 2, 1931, in an exhibition game in Chattanooga, Tennessee, a pitcher by the name of Jackie Mitchell struck out Babe Ruth and Lou Gehrig on six pitches. You'd think that a pitcher capable of such a feat would have a great future in the major leagues, but the hurler who humiliated Ruth and Gehrig never made it to the big time. You see, Jackie Mitchell was a girl.

RUNS HAVE ALWAYS been the trademark of the New York Yankees, and from August 2, 1931 to August 3, 1933 they really protected the franchise. During this period of just over two years, they played 308 games without being shut out in a single contest.

It was Lefty Grove who finally hung a goose egg on the Bombers from the Bronx. On August 3, 1933, the great Lefty broke the streak, but not the charm. From there on, the Yankees went the rest of the season without being shut out again.

Wild Horse of the Osage

Until the 1931 World Series started, Pepper Martin was just another ballplayer. Then he became metamorphosed into TNT on wheels.

In the first game, Martin garnered three solid hits off the great Lefty Grove, but Philadelphia won.

In the second tussle, Pepper smacked out two hits, stole two bags, and scored the only two runs for his team. The Cards won. Unquestionably, that victory was due to this amazing player who ran bases as if he had firecrackers in his shoes. He stretched a single into a daring two-bagger, then stole third by risking his neck in a reckless dive that barely beat the throw.

In the third encounter, Martin saved the day again.

But it was in the fifth game that Martin erupted like a volcano. Three scorching hits sparked off his bat; one was a terrific homer with one on. Altogether, the incredible kid drove in four runs to win the ballgame single-handed.

And to cap his one-man show, the Wild Horse of the Osage wound up the final fracas in Philadelphia in a full blaze of glory. It was the last half of the ninth. Two were out, but the tying runs were on base. Max Bishop lifted a high Texas-Leaguer. Everyone in the park held his breath as the Cardinal fireball sprinted in from deep center to make a thrilling one-handed catch for the final putout.

All St. Louis went delirious. Right then and there, Pepper Martin could have been elected governor of Missouri.

IN CLEVELAND on July 10, 1932, the Indians and the Athletics staged a farce in 18 acts which they deceptively labeled a ballgame.

The hero of this melange was Cleveland shortstop Johnny Burnett, who labored manfully in the batter's box to tag nine hits —the all-time major-league record for a single game.

Alas! Burnett's yeomanry naught availed. Cleveland lost by a score at once close and grotesque. At the end of 18 innings, the final count stood Philadelphia 18, Cleveland 17.

In the prodigious proceedings, some statistics are worthy of passing interest. The Indians scored 33 safe hits; the Athletics a mere 25. This totaled 58 safeties in a single game! The winning pitcher was reliever Ed Rommel, who allowed—hold on to your hat—29 hits!

Pinch Me for Luck

IN 1932, WHEN A state of emergency was deemed to exist, Brooklyn manager Max Carey used to call on his part-time outfielder Johnny Frederick. And most of the time, Frederick was Johnny-on-the-spot in the pinch.

On six occasions, he hammered the ball out of the park, setting a home-run mark for pinch-hitters.

E=MC²

Yankee second-baseman Tony Lazzeri had been getting a lot of publicity for his heady play. Lazzeri was so smart, the dailies proclaimed, that he never made an error of judgment on the field.

One morning, a newsman's panegyric to "Poosh-'em-up" Tony claimed that one of the main reasons he was so valuable a player was that he always knew what to do with the ball. In the game that afternoon, pitcher Lefty Gomez got himself into a bases-loaded jam with no one out. The infielders came in on the grass to make a play at the plate if the ball were to be hit directly at one of them.

The batter bounced Gomez's pitch back to the mound, a perfect home-to-first double play. But El Goofo whirled and threw the ball to Lazzeri, *who was standing halfway between first and second.* In shock, Tony held the ball as the batter reached first, and a run scored.

When he came to his senses, he charged to the mound and screamed at Gomez, "Why in hell did you throw the ball to me?"

Gomez coolly replied, "I've been reading in the papers how smart you are, and how you always know what to do with the ball. Well, I wanted to see what you would do with *that* one."

The Babe Calls His Shot

No one but the Babe would have been brash enough to try it. No one but the Babe would have gotten away with it. Set against the magnificent backdrop of the 1932 World Series, it provided one of the most dramatic climaxes ever recorded in baseball.

The Chicago fans had been riding the Babe unmercifully on that October 1, 1932. On the field, the Cubs themselves, stung by two defeats, were also taking it out on the Babe. The catcalls rose to a crescendo when the hulking, spindle-legged Babe stepped to the plate in the top half of the fifth. The score stood knotted at 4-4. There was one out, and the bases were empty.

Charlie Root split the plate with a sizzling beauty—a perfect strike. The Babe beat the ump to the gesture when he raised his right index finger in token of *Strike One!* The rabid crowd howled its glee.

Root wound up again and zipped another pitch down the groove. The Babe didn't wait for the umpire to call this one either. With a grin he raised two fingers in the air, calling *Strike 2!* on himself. From the stands, there issued an unholy roar of delight.

Ruth stepped out of the batter's box waiting for the hubbub to die down. The clatter only rose to new heights. In anticipation, the fans were tasting the joy of seeing the mighty Babe, the fabulous Sultan of Swat, strike out. Root proceeded to waste the next two pitches, trying to get the Babe to bite on a bad one.

It was then that Ruth made his immortal gesture of defiance. He lifted his hand and pointed—pointed toward the flagpole in deep center field. "That," said the gesture, "is where the next pitch is going to go."

And that is exactly where the ball went! On Root's next pitch, the Babe swung from his ankles and sent the ball soaring far into the center-field bleachers. It landed but a few feet to the side of the flagpole!

Stunned, the Chicago fans sat speechless as the grinning Babe cruised triumphantly around the bases.

ON APRIL 28, 1934, Goose Goslin of the Tigers was grooved for double trouble. In four consecutive times at bat, Goslin grounded into four twin killings. Then to make that day's performance glow with still more luster, Goslin booted a ball to hand Cleveland its only run of the game.

In spite of Goslin's rash of blunders, Detroit took the game 4-1.

King Carl Shows His Stuff

A smart gambling man wouldn't have risked a plugged nickel on Carl Hubbell's chances in the All-Star game on July 10, 1934. Anyway, not after the first two men came to bat in the first inning.

Charlie Gehringer, leading off for the American Leaguers, rapped a sharp single to center. Wally Berger, the Nationals' center-fielder, looking like anything but an all-star, bobbled the ball and Gehringer hitched up on second. Heinie Manush worked Hubbell for a walk. Now with two on and none out, the greatest concentration of slugging power ever assembled was lining up at the bat pile.

Coming up in order were Babe Ruth and Larrupin' Lou Gehrig. And if that weren't enough to frighten a pitcher out of the ballpark, following this gigantic pair were: Jimmy Foxx, whose 58 circuit-drives in the 1932 season fell just two short of the Babe's record; Al Simmons, twice the American League batting champ; and Joe Cronin, known as a tough man in the clutch.

The American League partisans were yelling for blood—Hubbell's blood. The Bambino settled into his familiar stance at the plate. Gabby Hartnett, the Nationals' catcher, started to walk toward the pitcher's box. Hubbell waved him back.

The imperturbable King Carl bore down. A few elliptical heaves and Babe Ruth had struck out!

But Hubbell was still in hot water—boiling hot. There were men on first and second as mighty Lou Gehrig came to bat. But Hubbell snaked his famous screwball over the plate and Larrupin' Lou, too, went down swinging.

Now Jimmy Foxx took his place in the batter's box. On the first pitch, Gehringer and Manush executed as neat a double steal as you'd want to see. A clean single could score two runs. Hubbell never turned a hair. Paying small heed to the men prancing on the bases, the masterful southpaw concentrated on the plate. And once again Hubbell came through. Jimmy Foxx fanned!

In the second inning, Carl didn't lose the touch. Al Simmons was swinging for the fences, but all he hit was air. Cagey Joe Cronin had no better luck. Catcher Bill Dickey nearly made it six in a row; but with two strikes on him, he singled. Dickey died at first, however, when Hubbell dispatched Lefty Gomez with three quickies right across the middle of the pan.

This was a day to remember; for against all the odds, the great King Carl had muffled five of the biggest guns in baseball— in a row!

ON AUGUST 4, 1934, Mel Ott, great outfield star of the New York Giants, became the first ballplayer of modern times to score six runs in a nine-inning game. To prove it wasn't an accident, Mel repeated the performance 10 years later.

Ott's sextette has since been equaled; but only Mel has two such scoring marathons to his credit.

The Dean of Dizziness

When Dizzy Dean first came to the majors, he used to leave his teammates dumbfounded with his brash conceit. Dizzy regarded himself as the best pitcher that ever lived, and he didn't mind telling that to anybody. And the funny part of it is, his boast wasn't far from the truth.

When Dean was just a rookie with the St. Louis Cards and had only been with the club a couple of weeks, the catcher, Jimmy Wilson, noticed that a couple of his rather expensive silk shirts were missing. The loss baffled Wilson until one fine morning he found Dizzy wearing one of his prized possessions. He grabbed the young hillbilly and was about to commit mayhem when Dean protested.

"Now, Jimmy," said Diz, "you're a pretty good sort, and you wouldn't want the greatest pitcher that ever lived to go around poorly dressed, would you? You'd want the very best kind of shirt for a pitcher who's better than Mathewson or Johnson, now wouldn't you, Jimmy? You know I'm better than those guys ever was, so why shouldn't I be wearing silk shirts?"

Wilson was so flabbergasted by Dean's sincere conceit that he couldn't help burst out laughing, as he asked, "How many shirts did you swipe, Dizzy?"

"Two," answered Dean. "Only two!"

Wilson then turned to the eccentric farm boy and said, "Dizzy, you know, come to think of it, two silk shirts really aren't enough for a pitcher who's greater than Johnson and Mathewson put together. Come around and I'll give you another one."

And a few days later, that's exactly what Dean did. He wasn't embarrassed in the least.

For make no mistake about it, Dean was one of the greatest hurlers of all time. Some pretty wise baseball men claim that he was definitely the greatest pitcher of his era. In his meteoric career, Dean performed miracles. He and his brother, Paul, boosted the St. Louis Cards from mediocrity to a World's Championship.

At the beginning of the 1934 season, Diz brashly announced that "Me and Paul is going to win 45 games." Diz was wrong. That season, he and his brother won 49 games.

When the pennant was clinched, Diz sounded off again, "Who's gonna win the World Series? Me 'n' Paul."

They did, too. In the seven-game series, Jerome Dean and his brother, Paul, won all four Cardinal victories.

Once the Dean duet pitched a doubleheader against the Dodgers. Dizzy hurled the first game, allowing the Dodgers three scattered hits. In the follow-up, Paul pitched a no-hitter.

The elder Dean, watching the proceedings, complained, "I wished I'da known Paul was goin' to pitch a no-hitter. I'da pitched one, too."

Like most of baseball's zanies, Dean was often a tremendous headache to his manager. But the Cardinal mentor, Frankie Frisch, had a knack for handling the great screwball.

Once, in the middle of a tough pennant drive, Manager Frisch slapped a midnight curfew on the team. Came 12 o'clock and four members of the team had not shown up at the hotel. Prominent among the missing was a fellow named Dean. When the four malefactors drifted back some time in the A.M., Frisch was waiting for them. After a few well-chosen words, Frisch fined the offenders $200 apiece. Dizzy drew a $400 impost.

Diz, brooding about the injustice of this inequality, went to Frisch next day and complained. "After all," he said, "it ain't like I was doin' something different than those other three guys. But you fined them just $200, and you threw a $400 fine at me. It just ain't right!"

Frisch threw an arm around Dean's shoulder. "Why, Diz," he remonstrated, "you're not the same as those other guys. You're the star of this team. You're the great Dizzy Dean. Everything about you has got to be bigger and better than anybody else. And that goes for the fines, too."

Diz hesitated a moment, and then his face lighted up. "Danged if you're not right, Frank," he said. Convinced, he went off beaming.

Though his big-league career saw him pitch only five full seasons, Dean built up an imposing record of 150 wins and 53 losses. In his five healthy years, 1932-1936, he averaged 24 victories a season—as good as the greatest in the Hall of Fame. And when Diz bragged that he was going to do something—he went ahead and did it.

One time, Diz promised a hospital ward of lame youngsters that he would fan the Giants' powerful Bill Terry the next day—with the bases full. In the ninth, the Giants were a run behind, there were two out, and men on first and second. Hughie Critz came to bat—a man Dean had little trouble handling all season. Diz walked him on four straight pitches.

Then Bill Terry strode to the plate. Dean looked at Terry and smiled. "I kinda hate to do this, Bill," he called, "but I done promised a bunch of kids I'd fan you with the bases full. That's why I walked Critz." Good as his word, he then proceeded to strike out Terry on three straight pitches.

Diz was only 26 when a broken toe, suffered in the All-Star game, caused him to change his style of pitching, a change that ruined his throwing arm.

So Dean broke into radio as a sports announcer. And what a broadcaster was ol' Diz. He could put reverse on the King's English, and curve a word around a microphone as readily as he had curved a ball around the plate. A fevered pitcher's brow was covered with *pressperation*; and with Dean many a player had *slud* into a base. If a fielder had *throwed* the ball a mite faster, the *empire* woulda called him out. Once Diz cheerfully announced, "and now the players have gone back to their *respectable* positions."

A group of shocked citizens protested to the radio station that Dizzy Dean was going to have all the school kids in Missouri talking like him if he was not removed from the airwaves. "Why, shore I say *ain't*," protested Dean, "but a lot of people who don't say *ain't*, ain't eatin'."

That retired the side. Diz stayed on the air. Whatever he was doing, it was pretty tough to knock Dizzy Dean out of the box.

WHEN CASEY STENGEL was managing the Dodgers, he started a

rookie hurler in one game. The first six opposing batters each took the youngster's first offering and blasted it for a safe hit.

Stengel called time to confer with the catcher. "Say, what's with him?" asked Casey, indicating the pitcher. "Has he got anything at all on the ball?"

"How the heck should I know?" shrugged the catcher. "After all, I ain't had my hands on a single ball he's thrown to the plate all afternoon."

Grand Master of the Grand Slam

You know how it is when the bases are loaded and everyone and his brother-in-law is sitting on the edge of his seat yelling for a hit.

In a long career, Lou Gehrig, the Iron Horse, found himself face-up to quite a few such situations. How did Larrupin' Lou comport himself? Did he disappoint his fans? Not Lou. Twenty-three times Gehrig came through with a ringing circuit-clout to clear the bases.

Twenty-three home runs with the bases loaded! That's a record, son!

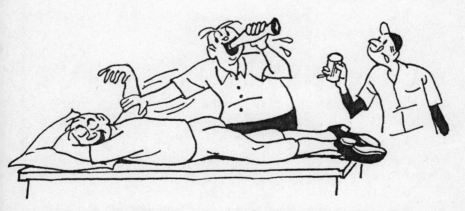

It's the Real Thing, or, The Rub That Refreshes

Ballplayers are notoriously superstitious, and many pitchers have a penchant for hypochondria. What happens when you put the two together? Listen to this one.

Guy Bush, a first-rate pitcher for the Cubs for more than a decade, once came to his trainer and asked what could be done for his sore arm. The trainer, Andy Lotshaw, rubbed up Bush's aching right arm with his secret liniment, and sent Bush on his way to the mound. Bush won.

By the time his next turn rolled around, Bush's arm was feeling much better, thank you, but he thought he'd take a little liniment just to be safe. He won again. This ritual continued for years; Bush swore by Lotshaw's secret cure.

When Bush finally retired, Lotshaw revealed the secret behind his secret cure. On that first day, when Bush had complained of a sore arm, Lotshaw had reached into his kit for liniment only to find he was all out. Thinking that Bush's ailment was located above the neck, the trainer reached for the first bottle of liquid he could lay his hands on. It was a bottle of Coca-Cola. And it was Coca-Cola that Lotshaw continued to rub on Bush's arm for the rest of his days with the Cubs.

CASEY STENGEL's hapless Brooklyn Dodgers had just dropped both ends of a twin bill. The Ol' Perfesser left the ballpark and headed straight for a barber shop, where he took a seat and told the tonsorialist:

"Once over and never mind cutting my throat. I may do that myself later this evening."

Bum Market

The Dodgers of the '30s were notorious card players, but all of a sudden their interest switched to Wall Street. Even the batboy was dabbling in the market. However, while the stocks went up, the team went down. When the Dodgers hit rock bottom, manager Casey Stengel decided he'd had enough.

After a particularly disastrous game, the Perfesser rushed into the clubhouse. "Hold everything, fellows!" he shouted excitedly. "I just got a hot tip on the New York Central Railroad!"

The players quickly crowded around the manager. "Are you sure?" they wanted to know. "Did you get your info from a good source?"

120

Stengel stared back at their anxious faces. "You're tootin' well right!" he yelled. "By the time I get finished shipping all you mugs back to the minors by New York Central tonight, they'll have enough dough to declare an extra dividend!"

Dizzy, Daffy, and Nutty

In 1934, the Dean brothers, pitchers Dizzy and Daffy, won 49 games between them to take the St. Louis Cardinals to the pennant. The following year, they teamed up to bring in 47 victories. They were tearing up the league.

One afternoon, Dizzy stopped by the Brooklyn clubhouse between games of a doubleheader to pay a visit to Dodger manager Casey Stengel.

"Are there any more at home like you and Paul?" Stengel asked Diz.

"We got another brother, Elmer," Dizzy replied, straight-faced. "He's down in Houston, burning up the league. You might get him cheap."

Stengel was so excited about this scoop that he told newspapermen he was going to bid for this third Dean boy. Only later did he learn that Elmer was burning up the Texas League as a peanut vendor in the Houston ballpark.

Iron Hands, Glass Jaw

One afternoon in 1935, the Cardinals were playing at the Polo Grounds, and taking a pretty good pasting from the Giants. Joe Medwick's indifferent play in left field had not made life any easier for the struggling Card pitchers.

After reliever Ed Heusser got the third out in a particularly inartistic inning, he returned to the dugout where he said a few words to Medwick about his iron hands. Medwick replied by belting Heusser in the jaw.

Heusser fell to the ground unconscious, and Medwick thus became the only man in baseball history to knock out his own relief pitcher.

AT THE BEGINNING of one season, Frankie Frisch, who was managing the St. Louis Cards, called a meeting of the rookies.

"There's one good way to get ahead in this game," he snapped. "Look around you. All of you pick some top-notcher on the team and follow his example."

That same afternoon during fielding practice, Frankie came across one of the rookies sprawled on the grass chewing a clover leaf, lackadaisically eyeing the proceedings.

The Fordham Flash blew a tonsil. "You lazy lunkhead," he shouted. "Only this morning I told you to pick one outstanding man on the club and do what he does. What do you think you're doing anyway?"

"Just like you said, Mr. Frisch," drawled the rookie. "I picked you."

Toe-Tapping Rhythm

Frenchy Bordagaray, Brooklyn outfielder in the '30s and '40s, had a knack for getting the two-base hit. He also had an unfortunate knack for getting picked off second immediately afterwards.

One afternoon, Dodger first-base coach Casey Stengel called time and ran out to the keystone, where the Frenchman stood after one of his typical two-baggers.

"Listen, Frenchy," Casey said, "this time I want you to stand on second until the batter actually hits the ball. Don't take a lead, don't even move six inches from the bag. Understand?"

"Certainly, Mr. Stengel," Frenchy replied.

Moments later, the pitcher whirled and fired a pick-off throw to second. The shortstop grabbed it, put the tag on Bordagaray, and sent the Frenchman trotting back toward the dugout.

"What happened?" the disgusted Stengel demanded as Bordagaray passed him.

"I haven't the slightest idea, Boss. I did just like you told me. I was standing there tapping my foot on the bag, waiting for the next batter to bang one."

"Then how did the shortstop manage to put you out?" Casey asked.

"I don't know," the Frenchman replied, throwing up his hands in defeat. "He must have put the tag on me between taps."

The Babe Bows Out

Well before the 1935 season began, Babe Ruth's golden career had begun to tarnish. Plagued by age and personal problems, the legendary Yankee slugger had become little more than a curiosity piece when he was traded to the Boston Bees. By mid-May of that year, the man who in 1927 had hit 60 homers was batting a dismal .179, and he was spending most of his time on the bench.

On May 25, 1935, the 40-year-old Bambino took the field against the Pirates in Pittsburgh. On his first trip to the plate, he cracked a long homer into the right-field stands. A few innings later, his bat sent another fastball soaring into the bleachers. Next time up, Ruth banged out a single that scored a run.

When the Babe stepped to the plate again late in the game, the fans were clamoring for another four-bagger. The old Sultan of Swat dug in, then brought the crowd to its feet with a towering blast to right that went clear out of Forbes Field. No one had ever hit a ball over those right-field stands before.

As Ruth rounded the bases, few could guess that this homer, number 714, would be his last. But the three home runs he hit that day were a fitting finale to a career without equal in baseball.

The Gotham Game

1936-1960

In 1936, Ruth was gone, and Gehrig had little time left. The Yankees had fallen short of the pennant the last three years. Murderers' Row was a thing of the past, and the Yanks needed a new slugger to lift them once again to the top.

Came a kid named Joe DiMaggio from San Francisco to fill the role. That year, the new young star hit .323, drove in 125 runs, and led the Yanks to a World Series victory over the Giants.

This "subway series" was the first of 10 which were to be played over the next two decades. The Bronx Bombers won nine of these meetings with their rivals from Manhattan and Brooklyn, losing only to the Dodgers in 1955.

Of the 50 pennants won between 1936 and 1960, a resounding 29 were captured by the three Gotham clubs. The Yanks continued to maul their American League opposition until 1965; but New York City's domination of baseball ended in 1957, when the Dodgers and Giants moved out to the West Coast.

Yet New York's preeminence was not the whole story of this 25-year period. Other stars besides DiMaggio arrived to replace the heroes of old. There was Bob Feller, then Ted Williams, and then Stan Musial. And from 1947 on, there came a succession of great black stars.

Jackie Robinson and Larry Doby were the first of this crop; Roy Campanella, Don Newcombe, and Monte Irvin followed on their heels. Willie Mays, Henry Aaron, Ernie Banks, and Roberto Clemente also broke in at this time and continued as top-flight performers for a long time.

Oh, Those Bases on Balls

In 1936, in his first big-league appearance, a 17-year-old kid from Van Meter, Iowa, named Bob Feller struck out 15 St. Louis Browns. A few weeks later, the same kid struck out 17 Philadelphia A's to tie the record then held by Dizzy Dean.

Though he won the game by a score of 5-2, Rapid Robert's performance could hardly be described as artistic. He walked nine men, hit a tenth, and allowed nine A's to steal bases, for Bob just didn't know how to pin a runner to the bag.

Two years later, when Feller whiffed 18 Tigers to break his own record, he walked seven men. This time his wildness was fatal and cost him the ballgame, 4-1.

Oddly, in 1969, when Steve Carlton broke Feller's mark by fanning 19 Mets, he too lost the game. In Carlton's case, the culprit was not wildness but the volatile gopher ball. Ron Swoboda hit a brace of homers that gave the overmatched Mets a 4-3 victory.

IT DOESN'T OFTEN happen in the majors that a man bats twice in the same inning. But when a man bats twice in one inning and hits each time for extra bases, that's really something.

Yet on August 25, 1936, three Bees accomplished this baseball rarity. In the first stanza of a game against the Cards, Eugene Moore, Tony Cuccinello, and Baxter Jordan each batted twice. They each hit two doubles.

What's in a Name?

In 1927, Pete Jablonowski came to the majors as a pitcher with the Cincinnati Reds. Over the next six years, he toiled with little distinction in the uniforms of three other clubs—the Cleveland Indians, the Boston Red Sox, and the New York Yankees.

In 1933, journeyman Jablonowski was sent down to the minors. In six years in the big time, he had compiled a less than dazzling record of 17 wins and 19 losses.

While in the minors, Jablonowski decided to change his name. Maybe he was just tired of waking up the morning after he pitched, picking up the paper, looking in the box scores, and seeing his name printed as J'b'n'ski.

Whatever the reason, when he changed his name legally to Peter Appleton, his pitching picked up. In 1936, he was brought back to the majors by the Washington Senators. Where Pete Jablonowski might have failed, Pete Appleton had a fine 14-9 season.

An Elite Club

Tony Lazzeri had what it takes! On May 24, 1936, the great Yankee second-sacker slammed two grand-slam homers in the same game, the first to accomplish this feat.

Amazingly enough, after Poosh-'em-up Tony made his wonderful record, five other American League sluggers performed the same spectacular feat, and so did a National League pitcher. In 1939, Jim Tabor of the Boston Red Sox celebrated the 4th of July by exploding for a brace of four-baggers, each drive clearing filled bases. Seven years later, on July 27, 1946, Rudy York of the Red Sox did it again.

In 1961, the man of the hour was Oriole slugger Jim Gentile. Five years later, Atlanta pitcher Tony Cloninger turned the trick. And in 1968, the Tigers' Jim Northrup joined the elite, which was closed out by Frank Robinson of Baltimore in 1970.

A home run with the bases full is every ballplayer's dream. Yet seven men have hit not only one but two super-dupers in the same game! Truth can be stranger than dreams.

IN 1936, THE Brooklynites were losing game after game in a disastrous slump. One afternoon during pregame practice, Frenchy Bordagaray accidentally beaned manager Casey Stengel with a thrown ball. In order not to further upset the team's already frazzled nerves, Casey heroically kept his temper.

That day, while a lump grew in Brooklyn, the Dodgers won.

After the game, Frenchy buttonholed Stengel in the clubhouse. "Casey," he said, "I think we got the answer. Just for luck, let me hit you on the head before every game. Then maybe we'll keep on winning."

SMALL WONDER that Hubbell of the Giants was called "King Carl." Starting in 1936 and continuing through 1937, Hubbell pitched 24 wins in a row.

ON SEPTEMBER 11, 1936, Horace Lisenbee, hurling for the Athletics, made a pitching record for himself. In a spirit of unparalleled generosity, Horace allowed the opposing batters 26 hits. No pitcher in the modern era has ever allowed more safeties in a nine-inning game.

El Goofo the Great

In 13 years with the Yankees, Vernon Gomez seemed always good for a game or a laugh—generally both at the same time.

There was, for instance, the last game of the 1937 World Series when the Giants faced the Yankees. Gomez was working the Giant batters carefully, and had matters pretty well under control. In the fifth inning, an airplane winged low over the Polo Grounds. Lefty forgot completely about the ballgame. With his mouth agape, he dreamily watched the aircraft until it flew out of sight behind the packed grandstand. Then, suddenly aware of the umpire's shout to play ball, Lefty nonchalantly stepped to the mound and finished the inning.

When he returned to the bench, he found manager Joe McCarthy in a towering rage. "Why, you blankety-blank screwball," yelped Joe. "Keep your mind on the game! With you daydreaming like that, I'm surprised they didn't start knocking the ball out of the park."

Gomez turned a slow and lofty stare toward the angry pilot. "Izzatso?" he queried. "I had a-hold of the ball all the time I was watching the plane, didn't I? How could they knock it out of the park?"

Lefty was a real aviation bug. His eyes would pop every time he drove past an airport. He was quite willing to go up in any old crate, even if it were held together with the proverbial chewing gum and baling wire.

One year, Joe McCarthy forbade Gomez to go up in the air. A few days later, McCarthy happened to look up. In the sky, he saw an airplane going through the most hair-raising stunts.

At dinner, Joe went over to Lefty's table. "Say," he said. "You should have been around this afternoon. You missed a real crackpot flier. Some people don't care a nickel for their lives. He was doing the worst lunatic stunts. . . ."

"You mean that bright red biplane?" asked Gomez.

"That's the one," said McCarthy. "It would have taught you a lesson. I hope you saw it."

"Well, not exactly," replied Gomez. "I was in it."

Though Gomez was a great hurler, McCarthy always felt that he was too frail. "Lefty," said Marse Joe at the tail-end of one season, "try to put on some weight this winter. Why, if you had another 15 to 20 pounds of meat on you, you'd make them forget every lefthander that ever tossed a ball."

This time, Gomez took McCarthy's advice to heart. The pitcher made the gaining of weight his winter project. After stuffing himself with all kinds of rich food, he checked in the following season with 20 additional pounds distributed over his angular frame. But somehow, the southpaw had one of his poorer seasons.

One day, when the schedule was nearly over, Gomez went up to McCarthy. "Joe," he said sadly, "you told me if I put on weight I'd make 'em forget every lefthander that ever pitched. You're probably right! Trouble is, when they start forgetting lefthanders, they'll most likely forget Gomez, too."

Vernon Gomez was far more than a goof. He was a great pitcher. Hurling 13 years for the Yanks, Gomez won 198 games. Pitching in four World Series, Lefty hurled six games to a decision—and won every one!

Fanned in Boston

Dizzy Dean was never hesitant about putting his money where his mouth was—and with ol' Diz's mouth, that's saying a lot.

Diz had a friend named Johnny Perkins who worked in a St. Louis nightclub, and occasionally Perkins followed the Cards on their road trips. On the train up to Boston early in 1937, Perkins bet Diz that he couldn't strike out the Bees' rookie Vince DiMaggio the first time he came up.

Dean did manage to fan DiMaggio, and from the bench, Dizzy signaled to Perkins that he'd go double or nothing on

Vince's next time up. Perkins agreed, and again Dean won the bet.

The same wager held on DiMaggio's third trip, and once again Dean took more of Perkins' money and DiMaggio's pride. As Vince came to the plate for the fourth time, he had no idea that he was a pawn in this game of high finance. He bore down and at last got a piece of the ball, lifting a high foul pop in back of the plate.

Diz ran toward home screaming at his catcher, Bob Ogrodowski, "Let it go, let it go!" Fortunately for Dean, the ball hit the screen on its downward arc, and the catcher couldn't lay his mitt on it for a putout. Then Diz went back to the mound and fanned DiMaggio for the fourth straight time.

OVER FOUR GAMES in 1938, Boston Red Sox third-baseman Pinky Higgins made 12 consecutive hits. It seemed like a record that would hold up for all time. But 14 years later, Detroit first-baseman Walt Dropo also got 12 straight hits, and he improved upon Higgins' performance by accomplishing the feat in only three games.

Two in a Row!

Perhaps the greatest pitching performance of all time was the pitching of two consecutive no-hit no-run games by Johnny

Vander Meer, the wonder boy of the Cincinnati Reds.

On June 11, 1938, Johnny pitched against the Boston Bees on his home ground and retired his opponents with only 28 men facing him. Only three men reached first base, all on walks.

Four days later, Vander Meer hurled against the Dodgers. The game took place in Brooklyn on the night when Ebbets Field first saw night baseball. But night or day, moon or sun, the Cincinnati southpaw kept mowing 'em down. He allowed eight men to reach first on free passes, but no man to tally.

If ever some young fellow gets to looking about for a record to beat, here's one to pitch for.

LEFTY GOMEZ's hitting was execrable. He just couldn't seem to follow the ball. And when he had to bat against Bob Feller one dark, overcast afternoon, he was totally lost.

Now Bob Feller's bullet-ball was a mean thing for a batter to face even when visibility was at its best. But when the day was gray, it took something like radar to locate the streaking pellet.

In the shadows of that gray afternoon, the Cleveland speedballer set down one Yankee batsman after another. Late in the game, as the gloom grew even darker, Lefty Gomez came to bat. Before he stepped into the batter's box, Lefty reached into his back pocket, pulled out a book of matches, lit one, and held it over his head.

"Cut the comedy!" growled the ump. "D'yuh think that match'll help you see Feller's fast one?"

"Shucks, that's not what I've got in mind," replied Gomez. "What I want to make sure of is that Feller sees me!"

Aw, Let Me Hit the Ball

On June 16, 1938, Jimmy Foxx stood in the batter's box six times, yet the official records do not credit him with a single time at bat! For on that day, opposing pitchers presented the Red Sox slugger with six bases on balls, a major-league record.

Jimmy led both leagues in batting that year, and knocked

in 175 runs. It's easy to see why pitchers were plenty afraid of the big, bad Foxx!

BE IT EVER so humble, there's no place like home. After the 1938 season, Tiger slugger Hank Greenberg certainly subscribed to that sentiment. Of the 58 homers Hammerin' Hank collected, 39 were poled in Detroit's Briggs Stadium.

Yes, But...

A reporter once asked the late Miller Huggins what a ballplayer needed most when he was deep in a slump.

"A string of good alibis," was Huggins' unhesitating reply.

It took a master of the art of alibi, Bobo Newsom, to talk himself out of the hot spot in which he once found himself. Hurling for the Browns against a hard-hitting Philadelphia team, Newsom was sweating out a massacre. When the Browns came off the field to bat in their half of the seventh, the score stood 15-0 in favor of the Athletics.

"Gosh, Bobo," said a teammate, as Newsom came into the dugout, "they're really beatin' you today."

"Ah, nuts!" replied Newsom. "How d'ya expect a pitcher to win games if his club don't give him any runs?"

Take a Back Seat, Sonny

Who pitched the fastest fastball? Some people say Bob Feller, others say Sandy Koufax, and Nolan Ryan has his supporters, too. But ask an oldtimer for his opinion, and he'll invariably say Walter Johnson.

The Big Train was a gentle, exceedingly modest man, but he was not without pride. In 1939, more than a decade after Johnson had retired, he went to spring training with the Senators as a radio announcer. In camp, everyone was talking about Roberto Ortiz, a Cuban rookie with blinding speed.

Ortiz was a bit of a blusterer, and one day he decided to show the old master how it was done. He began warming up right in front of Johnson's seat in the stands. Johnson watched Ortiz rear back and fire about 15 minutes. Then the Big Train took off his coat and tie, climbed over the railing, and called over Walter Millies, a Washington catcher.

The 52-year-old Johnson began warming up alongside Ortiz, and soon started to time his pitches so they left his hand at the same moment Ortiz's pitches were leaving *his* hand. Johnson's cannonballs were smacking into Millies' glove before Ortiz's pitches arrived in his catcher's mitt! Finally, the Cuban stopped throwing and just watched Johnson smoke away.

When asked about this contest later in the day, Johnson said, "I couldn't resist the temptation. May the good Lord forgive me."

134

Arriba! Arriba!

In addition to managing the Dodgers, Yankees, and Mets, Casey Stengel also led the Boston Bees between 1938 and 1943. One spring, during an exhibition tour south of the border, as the Braves' bus made its way to the hotel, Casey found the streets of Monterrey, Mexico, lined with cheering crowds.

"Listen to 'em!" Casey exclaimed as he looked out the window at the arm-waving, flower-tossing throng. "There'll be a million fans today at the ballpark!"

When the bus pulled up in front of the hotel, a young Mexican was there to greet them. "Señor Stengel," he said politely, "I am assigned to be your guide while you are here in Monterrey."

"Say, ain't this a wonderful greeting!" the manager answered happily. "I didn't know you people were so crazy about baseball."

The guide stared down at his shoes in embarrassment. "Oh, it's not the players they're cheering," he replied sheepishly, "it is just that they have never seen a Greyhound bus before."

The Splendid Splinter

Heading into the final weekend of the 1941 season, Ted Williams looked like a sure bet to become the first man in over a decade to hit .400. But in Saturday's game against the Philadelphia A's, the Boston star was whiffed three times by rookie Roger Wolff, and his average dipped to .3996.

On Sunday, manager Joe Cronin asked Williams whether he wanted to play in the doubleheader. If Ted sat it out, Cronin reminded him, his average would be rounded off in the record books to an even .400. But Williams said, "I'll play. I don't want anyone to say I got in through the back door."

Responding to the pressure, Ted knocked out four hits in the first game, and two more in the second. He had cleared the .400 hurdle by a full six points.

No one else has attained a .400 batting average since Williams posted his .406 in 1941. Indeed, no one even seriously challenged .400 for the next 17 years, until a 39-year-old outfielder swatted .388. His name? Ted Williams.

And Pepper Was Right!

During spring training in 1940, Cardinal manager Ray Blades called the squad in for a general meeting. When Ray asked if anyone had any suggestions for improving the training methods, Pepper Martin stood up. The 36-year-old veteran pointed out that the Yanks, who were training on the other side of Fort Lauderdale, were holding only one workout a day.

"The Yanks keep winning pennants," Pepper said, "so maybe they're doing something right, and we should follow them."

"No," Blades replied, "we're going to stick to two workouts a day. The Yankee record should be an incentive for us. If we want to be like the Yankees, we'll just have to work twice as hard as they do. Okay, Pepper?"

"Yeah," said Martin. "But I got a jackass back home in Oklahoma, and you can work him from sunup to sundown and he ain't never gonna win the Kentucky Derby."

BACK IN '41, the Yankee Clipper was really clipping 'em. In 56 straight games during that summer, DiMaggio was never shut out of the hit column!

It was on May 15, 1941, that Joltin' Joe started his socking spree. Before the string was snapped on July 17, DiMag had hit 73 moundsmen for 91 safeties. Of these, 35 were extra-base blasts. Sixteen hits went for doubles; four for three-baggers; and 15 for home runs. His batting average for the 56-game streak was a juicy .408.

A ROOKIE once approached Cardinal manager Billy Southworth and asked complainingly why he was kept on the bench.

"What have you got against me?" said the kid. "Yesterday you saw me rap out two doubles and a triple. How can you keep a .400 hitter like me on the bench?"

"The trouble," answered Southworth, "is that you're also a .400 fielder."

ONLY EIGHT hitters in modern major-league history have batted .400 for a full season. Here they are:

1901 Napoleon Lajoie	Philadelphia Athletics	.422
1911 Joe Jackson	Cleveland Naps	.408
1911 Ty Cobb	Detroit Tigers	.420
1912 Ty Cobb	Detroit Tigers	.410
1920 George Sisler	St. Louis Browns	.407
1922 Ty Cobb	Detroit Tigers	.401
1922 George Sisler	St. Louis Browns	.420
1922 Rogers Hornsby	St. Louis Cardinals	.401
1923 Harry Heilmann	Detroit Tigers	.403
1924 Rogers Hornsby	St. Louis Cardinals	.424
1925 Rogers Hornsby	St. Louis Cardinals	.403
1930 Bill Terry	New York Giants	.401
1941 Ted Williams	Boston Red Sox	.406

It is also notable that only two hitters of modern times have had three .400 seasons—one player in each league: Cobb in the American League and Hornsby in the National League.

There's Only One Catch...

The years 1941-45 were lean years for baseball. Most of the quality players were in the service, and each club had to stock its roster with washed-up veterans and green kids.

At one tryout camp during the war, a kid walked up to

manager Charley Grimm of the Chicago Cubs and said, "I'm 4F, and I can hit like Ted Williams, throw as fast as Dizzy Dean, and play the outfield better than Joe DiMaggio."

"You're nuts," said Grimm.

"Sure—that's why I'm 4F."

Foul Play

Though Luke Appling made it to Cooperstown on the strength of his .310 lifetime average and his 21 years as the shortstop of the Chicago White Sox, he deserved a niche in the Hall of Fame merely for his uncanny ability to hit foul balls.

In years past, the Yankees were rather miserly when it came to doling out free passes to the visiting team. When Lucius learned that his request for two passes to the ballgame had been denied, he knew how to exact sweet revenge. He stepped into the cage for batting practice, and proceeded to ram 25 straight foul balls into the stands, at $2 per ball. Naturally, these balls were supplied by the Yanks. When Yankee officials upstairs realized that Appling was making them pay over $50 for the two passes they denied him, they immediately sent down word that he could have his free tickets.

On another occasion, Appling waited for the game to start before tormenting the Yanks. Coming to bat in the bottom of the first on a hot day in Chicago, Luke was up against Red Ruffing, with two on and two out. The Yankee ace zipped in two quick strikes, and Appling was in the hole. He fouled off the next four pitches, then took a called ball one. Then he fouled off six more.

Ruffing issued ball two, followed by ball three. The next 14 pitches came in over the plate, and Appling fouled off every one. At last, thoroughly exasperated, Ruffing gave Appling ball four.

The next batter to face the arm-weary pitcher was Mike Kreevich, and Mike doubled to clear the bases.

When manager Joe McCarthy lifted Ruffing for a reliever, Red left the mound screaming at Appling, who was sitting placidly in the dugout. "You did it! You did it with those *#%&@ foul balls!"

THERE MUST HAVE BEEN some magnetism in Eddie Joost's glove that attracted horsehide, for everything that came off the bats of the opposing team on May 7, 1941, simply scurried his way.

Eddie was sure a busy man that afternoon. Playing in a Cincinnati uniform, Eddie cavorted around shortstop, handled 20 balls, and made nine putouts and ten assists for a record of 19 accepted chances. On such a busy afternoon, who could blame him for turning in one solitary error?

The One That Got Away

From the beaches of Coney Island to the garbage banks of Gowanus, October 5, 1941, will always be remembered in Brooklyn as Black Sunday. For on this tragic afternoon, the ghost of a World's Championship fled from Flatbush astride a skittish baseball—the fateful ball that broke away from catcher Mickey Owen in the ninth.

To that point in the 1941 Series, Fate hadn't been kind to Dem Bums. The day before, Freddy Fitzsimmons, fat and 40, had been pitching the game of his life, holding the Yankees to four scraggly hits in seven innings. Then a fierce line drive caught Freddy in the knee and put him out of the game. Hugh Casey went in to relieve, and the Bronx Bombers immediately solved him for two runs—just enough to win.

But the Dodgers had plenty of fight; and on this memorable Sunday, they had bounced back to overcome a three-run Yankee lead. Coming into the ninth, the Brooklynites were ahead 4-3. Hugh Casey was on the hill again, turning in a masterful relief performance. Two were out, the bases empty, when Tommy Henrich stood at the plate for the Yanks. Fireman Casey worked him carefully. There were two strikes against Henrich when Casey wound up and delivered his Sunday pitch—a magnificent fast-breaking curve. Henrich whipped his bat around—and missed! Plate umpire Goetz jerked his thumb upward for *Strike 3*, and an ear-splitting roar went up from the stands.

That did it! That put the bold, battling Bums even up at two games apiece with the Yankees! Oh, boy! We'll moider 'em tomorrow!

But wait!—out of the bleacher woodwork, the Flatbush jinx had crawled again! The roar died in Brooklyn throats as they saw catcher Mickey Owen whip off his mask, swing around to his right, and start chasing after a dribbling speck of white. He had dropped the third strike! Henrich had been given a new lease on life. Now he had to be thrown out at first!

Mickey couldn't recover the pill in time, and Henrich made it. This brief reprieve gave the Yankee heavies another chance to unlimber and swing into action. Joe DiMaggio jolted a hard single to left. King Kong Keller, laughing off a count of two strikes, laid one up against the right-field fence for two bases, scoring Henrich and DiMag. Casey walked Bill Dickey to get at second-sacker Joe Gordon. But Gordon blasted a two-bagger, driving Keller and Dickey across for two more tallies. The unhappy fireman finally put out the blaze by disposing of Yankee pitcher Johnny Murphy.

The Dodgers, utterly crushed, could do nothing in their half of the ninth. The final score stood New York 7, Brooklyn 4. Instead of even-up, the Yanks led three games to one.

To all intents and purposes, that ended the Series. The Yankees' win on the next day merely placed the official seal on an accomplished fact.

Maybe the Yankees would have won anyway, but out in Brooklyn, any Dodger fan will tell you how a World's Championship positively slipped through Mickey Owen's fingers.

Putting Things in Perspective

Ted Williams was the last ballplayer on record to hit over .400, and he may be the last *ever* to do so, in this era of transcontinental travel and night games. After attaining a .406 mark in 1941, the Boston star was asked how he felt.

"Well," he said, "suppose your boss gave you ten jobs to do and you only did four of them right. How would you feel?"

ON THE 13th of September, 1942, Lennie Merullo shoulda stood in bed. On that day, in one onerous inning, the Cubs' shortstop accepted four fielding chances and bobbled every one!

Oh! Oh! Oh! Oh!

Let Joe Do It

On June 17, 1943, the Red Sox were playing a doubleheader against the Athletics. In the seventh inning of the first game, the Bosox were standing at the short end of a 4-1 score, but had two men on base. Manager Joe Cronin sent pinch-hitter Joe Cronin in to bat.

Joe picked a good one, clouted it out of the park, and tied up the score, paving the way for a 5-4 Boston victory.

On that same afternoon, in the eighth inning of the second game, Joe Cronin again sent himself in to try his luck in the pinch. Joe didn't fail himself. He hit a homer again.

Take That!

Frenchy Bordagaray, the famed Dodger eccentric of the '30s and '40s, once got into a fierce dispute with an umpire. When the arbiter would not adjust his views to comply with those of Frenchy, Frenchy punctuated his argument by spitting in the ump's eye.

Frenchy found this a fitting climax to a difference of opinion with a man in blue, but the league regarded the matter more seriously. Bordagaray was fined $500 and suspended for 60 days.

When he learned of this action, the gallant Gallic allowed that he may have committed a breach in decorum. "Okay, maybe I did wrong to spit in the ump's eye," said Bordagaray. "But the penalty is a little more than I expectorated."

THE U.S. ARMY has a measuring device that can gauge the speed of a projectile. Put into use before a game in Cleveland, the gadget clocked Bob Feller's plate-scorcher at 98.6 miles per hour. That mark stood until 1974, when the California Angels' speedballer Nolan Ryan threw a pitch that was timed at 100.4 miles per hour!

DURING WORLD WAR II, Japanese soldiers were stung by the barbs of American troops, in particular by the placing of an indelicate imperative before the name of Emperor Hirohito.

Sitting in their foxholes, the Japanese would shout what they thought to be a fitting retort: "The hell with Babe Ruth!"

Indian Uprising

When the Yanks played the Indians on July 2, 1943, everything looked calm and peaceful for three innings. But in the fourth, the Indians suddenly went on the warpath and lambasted the enemy with everything and then some. By the time the eruption had subsided, a dozen Clevelanders had crossed the plate.

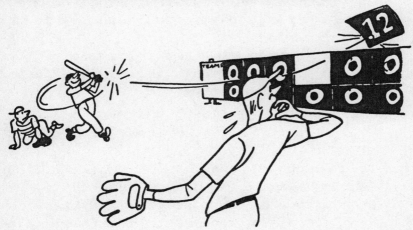

Then the Indians were sated and behaved like so many sleepy children. For the rest of the game, they didn't score a run. As for the Yanks, they never even got their bats warmed up. Cleveland's rookie hurler, Allie Reynolds, mowed them down with only three hits.

The Yanks had to wait four years to exact their revenge. In 1947, they acquired Reynolds from the Tribe, and he led them to the flag.

For Fast Relief, Take These Two

When Joe Nuxhall came in to face the Cardinals in the ninth inning on June 10, 1944, the Reds were trailing, 13-0. When Nuxhall walked off the mound, the score stood 19-0. This major-league debut was so harrowing that it took Nuxhall eight years to get his name in another major-league box score. But it's hard to blame the rookie for being a little shook up by his harsh introduction to the big time. Nuxhall was only 15 years old—the youngest major-leaguer ever.

Another man who had a rough initiation on the mound was Ernie Shore. In 1912, in his one and only inning of work for the New York Giants, the frantic freshman gave up eight hits and ten runs. But five years later, with the Boston Red Sox, Shore pitched the greatest game anyone has ever hurled in relief.

On June 23, 1917, the starting pitcher for the Sox was a fellow named George Herman Ruth. The star lefthander walked the first Washington batter on a close pitch, and proceeded to give the ump a very large and nasty piece of his mind. In turn, the ump gave Babe the thumb.

Shore was brought in, and on his first pitch the man on first was thrown out trying to steal. Shore went on to retire the next 26 men in order, for a perfect game.

Twilight of a Star

When the Red Sox traded Jimmy Foxx to the Cubs, injuries plus the ravages of time had reduced the great slugger to but a shell of his former self. Playing with pulled cartilage and a fractured rib, all the 35-year-old Foxx could collect for the Cubs was three homers and a sickly .205 batting average.

The following year, Jimmy left baseball to work for a Philadelphia oil company. But in 1944, the war-depleted Cubs asked him to give it another try, and for 15 games he did. The results were even more embarrassing: one base hit in 20 at-bats for an average of .050.

In 1945, the Cubs did not invite him back, but the Phillies did. The reason was obvious: the Cubs were on their way to a pennant, the Phillies on their way to the basement. Shuttling between first and third, Jimmy managed a respectable .268 in 89 games for the Phils.

Foxx was only playing out the string, but sometimes the once great have one last burst of greatness left in them. One day manager Ben Chapman was hard up for a pitcher, and remembering that Foxx had once done some hurling in his teens, he asked Jimmy to go out and give it a try.

"Okay, Ben," Foxx said, "but I don't think I can last more than five innings."

"If you can go five, that'll be a big help," Chapman replied.

So Foxx went out there, and all he did was throw a no-hitter for five innings! When he finally gave up a hit in the sixth, Chapman let him call it a day. The reliever held the Phils' lead, and pitcher Foxx scored his first big-league victory. He never played in another game.

Profiles in Courage

In 1945, Pete Gray and Bert Shepard left their marks as two of baseball's all-time greats. You never heard of them? Well, that's not altogether surprising, since outfielder Gray hit a mere .218 for the Browns, while pitcher Shepard only got into one game for the Senators.

These two men are all-time greats simply because they played in the major leagues. You see, Gray had only one arm, and Shepard only one leg.

Gray lost his arm at age six, but he was determined to be as good with his one arm as other kids were with two. Playing baseball after school, he learned how to slash at the ball with his one arm, punching line drives over the infield. When a fly ball came to him in the outfield, he would catch the ball in his glove, then flip the ball in the air while removing the glove with the stub of his right arm.

In 1944, playing for Memphis in the Southern Association, Pete hit .333, stole 68 bases, and even hit five homers. He was voted the league's MVP, and his contract was bought by St. Louis in 1945. Though Gray never became a star, he was an inspiration to thousands of crippled kids and wounded veterans home from the war.

One of these veterans was Lieutenant Bert Shepard. Before he enlisted in 1942, his ambition was to be a big-league pitcher. But in 1944, his P-38 was shot down over Germany and his right leg was mangled in the wreckage. German doctors had no choice but to amputate just below the knee.

When Shepard came back to the States, he was fitted with an artificial limb at Walter Reed Hospital. One week later, he walked into the Washington Senators' spring-training camp at College Park, Maryland, and asked for a tryout. He got one, and proved good enough to make the squad.

As the season progressed into July, Shepard had not yet appeared in a game. Senator owner Clark Griffith and manager Ossie Bluege didn't really have much faith in his ability, and preferred just to let the lieutenant pitch batting practice, for the benefit of other crippled servicemen who might be feeling a little sorry for themselves.

But one day in late July, the Senators quickly fell behind the Red Sox. As the Bosox continued parading around the bases, Bluege signaled the bullpen for Shepard. Shepard retired his first man for the final out of the inning, and went on to pitch four more innings of three-hit baseball, allowing only one run while striking out three. Soon after that appearance, Shepard's leg began bothering him again, and he had to go back to the hospital. Though he returned to the Senators later in the year, he never pitched again in the big time. But Lieutenant Shepard had achieved his lifelong ambition—to become a big-league pitcher.

Hot Ott Plots Pot

When Mel Ott was piloting the Giants, he bound his pitchers by an inflexible rule. They were never—but never—to put across a plate-splitter when the count was two strikes and no balls against the batter. For violating that edict, Ott once fined pitcher Bill Voiselle $500. After that, the Giant twirlers observed Ott's rule religiously.

Shortly after the Voiselle episode, a newcomer fresh from a Giant farm club was sent in as a relief pitcher. There were men on second and third, and a .300 hitter was at the plate.

The first two deliveries went for strikes. Heedful of Ott's rule, the rookie then prepared to waste one. But things can happen to the most careful pitcher, and the youngster's third one clipped the corner of the plate.

"Strike three!" announced the ump.

The kid pitcher grew pale. "No!" he yelled as he left the hill and rushed toward the umpire. "That was a ball! What are you trying to do, ruin me?"

The Element of Surprise

The Red Sox and the Cardinals had split the first six games of the 1946 World Series. In the bottom of the eighth inning of game seven, the score was knotted at 3-3. You couldn't ask for a more tense and evenly played Series.

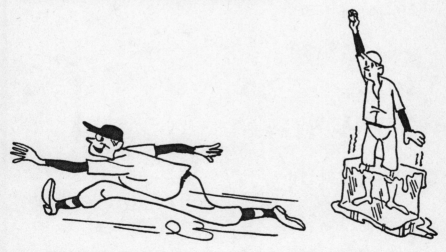

Sox reliever Bob Klinger came in to pitch the eighth inning. Enos Slaughter greeted Klinger with a single. The next Redbird batter, Whitey Kurowski, popped out trying to bunt Enos over into scoring position. Then Del Rice flied out to Ted Williams in left. When Harry Walker took two quick strikes, Cardinal fans started looking ahead to the ninth.

147

But on the next pitch, St. Louis manager Eddie Dyer flashed the hit-and-run sign. Slaughter took off with the pitch, and Walker drove the ball over second for a single. Sox center-fielder Leon Culberson raced in to pick up the ball, but it was clear that Slaughter would make third easily. Correctly, Culberson threw the ball in to the cutoff man, shortstop Johnny Pesky.

Imagine Pesky's surprise when with the ball in his hand he turned back toward the infield and saw Slaughter racing for the plate! The Sox shortstop was so utterly flabbergasted that for an instant he froze, unable to throw homeward.

That slight hesitation proved fatal to Boston hopes, for Slaughter scored from first on the single. His mad dash had put the Cards in front, 4-3, and that's the way the ballgame ended.

IN HIS EARLY big-league days, pitchers could play on one batting weakness of Yogi Berra: it was a cinch to make the Yankee catcher bite on the first pitch.

Once, with Berra about to take his turn at bat, Yankee manager Bucky Harris drew him aside and cautioned: "Now look, Yogi, don't always take your cut at the first one. Wait for a good one and think before you swing. The idea is to think! Now get in there and do what I tell you."

Yogi picked up his bat, pulled down his cap, and took his place in the batter's box. He didn't bite at the first one. The umpire called it a strike. The second one split the plate. Yogi never moved. The third pitch, too, was a sweet one, but Berra just watched it pass by.

Berra dragged his bat back to the dugout and dropped it on the pile. He walked over to Harris. "It's your fault," he said bitterly. "What do you expect? How can a guy think and hit at the same time?"

Only One Out Away

It was the ninth inning of the fourth game of the World Series, October 3, 1947, and all that stood between big Bill Bevens and baseball immortality was one out. One single, solitary out would give the lumbering Yankee righthander the first no-hit game in World Series history.

Bevens had plenty of stuff that afternoon, but he couldn't always control it. He had walked eight men. Two of these passes, blended with a sacrifice and a force play, had put a run across for the Dodgers in the fifth frame. But going into the ninth, it was indisputably a no-hit game, and the Yanks were still ahead by a score of 2-1.

With one out in the final stanza, Bevens, still a mite shy of control, walked Carl Furillo. Then Spider Jorgenson flied out. Two down and only one to go!

Pete Reiser, still limping from an ankle injury suffered the day before, went in to pinch-hit for the Dodgers' relief hurler, Hugh Casey. Bevens tried to get him to bite on some bad ones. No dice. The count went to three balls and no strikes. Now Bevens was faced with the unpleasant choice of grooving one for Pistol Pete or handing him a free pass. He looked toward the bench for instructions.

Manager Bucky Harris of the Yankees elected to violate the old baseball adage, "Never walk the winning run to first." He signaled Bevens to put Reiser on.

Now it was Burt Shotton's turn to do some master-minding

for the Brooklyn Dodgers. After sending in Eddie Miksis to run for the ailing Reiser, Shotton turned toward the bench. He jerked his thumb at Cookie Lavagetto.

A tremor of excitement passed through the Dodger dugout. Shotton was sending in the once able but now fast-fading Cookie as a pinch-hitter. And to take the place of Eddie Stanky, Brooklyn's reliable lead-off man! Doubt in the dugout was so thick you could slice it with a fungo bat.

Lavagetto stepped into the batter's box, and Bevens buckled grimly to his task. If he could only get over this last hurdle, World Series glory would be his. Lavagetto pulled nervously at his belt.

Big Bill wound up and scorched one straight down the slot. Lavagetto swung—and missed! Only two strikes to go! Now to tempt him to swing at a bad one. The big righthander threw it high and outside. Lavagetto swung again—and connected!

Tommy Henrich in right field started running at the sound of ball meeting bat. He arrived at the concrete wall just a fraction of a second after the horsehide. Taking the ball on the first bound, Henrich flung it homeward. It reached the plate a bare second after the flying spikes of Eddie Miksis clicked across with the winning run.

Lavagetto had come through with the Dodgers' only hit of the afternoon. Though Cookie was the toast of a delirious Brooklyn, many fans who were thrilled no end by the great pinch-hit were also mindful of the tragic disappointment of big Bill Bevens, who had come within two strikes of a World Series no-hitter and everlasting fame.

He Put His Money Where His Mouth Was

In 1947, the St. Louis Browns were buried deep in the cellar, and radio announcer Dizzy Dean didn't try to gild the stinkweed. When a Brownie bobbled a ball, Dean groaned in agony, spurning the old broadcaster's alibi of the "bad hop." If a pitcher was getting bombed, Diz didn't lather on about "all those Texas-Leaguers and seeing-eye grounders." Indeed, Dean proclaimed that he could pitch better than nine of the ten men on the Browns' staff.

As the season wore on and Brownie fortunes failed to improve, several players' wives became exceedingly disgruntled over Dean's unvarnished reportage in re their hubbies. "If that Dean thinks he's so great," the wives complained to Browns' president Bill DeWitt, "then why doesn't he go out there and pitch himself?"

DeWitt thought this was a marvelous idea. Attendance had been sagging at Sportsman's Park, and the prospect of ol' Diz on the hill would be sure to pack in the customers. The only trouble was that Dean hadn't pitched since 1941, and hadn't pitched without pain in his right arm since 1937. And that was ten years back.

DeWitt called Dean and made his proposal. Diz picked up the gauntlet, and readied himself for the big day. On September 28, he stepped on the field as the Browns' starting pitcher against the Chicago White Sox.

Dean struggled through the first three innings without giving up a run. When he came to bat in the bottom of the third, he surprised even himself by smacking a single. But while running to first, he felt a muscle pop in his leg.

He pitched the top of the fourth on sheer guts and savvy, then called it a day. In four full innings, Diz had given up no runs and only three hits.

"I said I could pitch as good as most of these fellows," Dean told newsmen after the game, "and I can. But I'll be doggoned if I'm ever going to try this stunt again. Talking's my game now, and I'm just glad that the muscle I pulled wasn't in my throat."

IN 1947, RALPH KINER of the Pirates slugged out a total of 51 four-baggers. So did Johnny Mize. In 1948, Mize of the Giants hit 40 circuit-drives. Kiner obliged by hitting exactly the same number.

Here's the greatest Alphonse-Gaston act in baseball history.

A Horse Gives Leo the Lip

Leo Durocher's favorite baseball joke is the one about a horse that trotted up to him in the dugout and said he wanted to play with the Dodgers. Leo obliged and went to the mound to pitch a few, while the horse stepped to the plate with a bat between his teeth. Leo delivered, and the horse smacked one out of the ballpark.

"Not bad," Leo told the horse, "but can you field?"

The horse trotted to the outfield. Leo fungoed a few, the nag snared each drive cleanly between his teeth, then dropped the ball and kicked it crisply and accurately back to the infield.

"Pretty good," the Lip had to admit. "But one more thing: Can you run?"

"Run?" the horse whinnied. "If I could run, would I be here looking for a job?"

RED JONES, an American League umpire in the late 1940's, was being given the business one day by the Chicago bench jockeys. Over and over again, the word "meathead" wafted from the dugout toward home plate. At last, Jones could take no more, and sent everyone on the bench in for an early shower.

The next day, as Jones came out on the field to start the proceedings, he passed in front of the White Sox dugout. "Oh, Mr. Umpire," the players cooed in unison, "you won't have any trouble with us today."

"That's nice," said Red, "but what makes you so sure?"

Then came the chorus: "We can't call you meathead today because it's Friday."

IN 1948, THE YANKS, the Red Sox, and the Indians were locked in a down-the-final-stretch struggle. The Bombers were battling the Bosox in a tough one. In the top of the tenth, the score stood 6 to 6. The Yanks had the bases full, with two out. There was a tense hush as Joe DiMaggio stepped into the batter's box.

Earl Caldwell, Boston's 43-year-old relief ace, wound up and let fly. DiMag lashed out with his bat and sent a tremendous drive roaring out to left field. It cleared the wall—inches on the wrong side of the foul line!

With sighs of relief, the Beantown rooters settled back into their seats. In the press box, a writer expressed everybody's feelings when he said, "You don't hit two balls that hard in one time at bat."

He was wrong, because you do if your name is DiMaggio. The Yankee Clipper lashed into Caldwell's very next delivery. The center-fielder got only a glimpse of the ball as it landed high in the bleachers.

The Oldest "Rookie"

Because of the major leagues' color barrier, not broken until 1947, Satchel Paige became the oldest rookie in baseball history. When he first took the mound for the Indians on July 9, 1948, Satch was listed as 42 years old, but may well have been closer to 50. He had been a professional hurler for more than 25 years, and had chalked up more than 2,000 victories.

White ballplayers had known about Satch for years. Many major-league stars had faced Paige in barnstorming games, and few had fared well. In one game, Paige fanned Rogers Hornsby five times; in other games, he put down Jimmy Foxx on strikes three times, and Charlie Gehringer the same number of times.

In 1934, after Dizzy Dean concluded his 30-win season by adding two more in the World Series, Satch took him on in a 13-inning duel. Paige won, 1-0.

Even as an over-the-hill rookie in 1948, Old Satch showed white America something of his former greatness. On his first trip to the mound as a Cleveland starter, he threw a three-hit shutout.

Paige pitched 178 games in the big leagues before retiring after the 1953 season. But he kept on pitching, often in the old backwater haunts where he had played at his peak. Then in 1965, as a publicity gimmick, the Kansas City A's signed Satch to a player's contract. Not long thereafter, the ancient Paige—admittedly 59 and perhaps 70—toed the rubber as the starting pitcher against the Boston Red Sox. In three innings, he allowed no runs and only one hit.

In 1971, Satchel Paige was at last accorded recognition for his accomplishments, taking his rightful place alongside Johnson, Young, and Mathewson in baseball's Hall of Fame.

Boy Wonder Makes Good

It's hard to imagine anyone having a better year than Lou Boudreau had in 1948. He fielded his shortstop position brilliantly, he hit .355, and he managed his Cleveland Indians to a pennant and a World Series victory.

Six years earlier, in 1942, Boudreau had become the boy wonder of baseball as he took the Cleveland helm at the age of 24. But in those six years, he had not even come close to bringing Cleveland its first flag since 1920. Owner Bill Veeck let Boudreau know how impatient he was becoming, and that 1948 might well be Lou's last year in Cleveland if he did not bring the team to the finish line in first place.

Well, when the season ended, Lou had brought his Indians into first—but the only trouble was that the Boston Red Sox were there, too. A one-game playoff would decide the pennant-winner.

Boudreau came to bat in the first inning at Fenway Park and parked a pitch over the left-field fence. But the Sox quickly tied it up at 1-1, and that's the way it stood when Lou came to the plate again to lead off the fourth. Boudreau singled, and moved to second on Joe Gordon's hit. Both then scored on Ken Keltner's three-run homer.

The game was now on ice, but Lou was taking no chances. He added another homer and another single, and on his last at-bat, was intentionally walked. In the most important game of his life, Boudreau had gone 4-for-4.

After the drama of the playoff, the Series was a cakewalk: the Indians beat the Braves in six games.

IN THE THIRD INNING of a game played on September 11, 1949, an assortment of Yankee pitchers gave up 11 free passes. But if any team in baseball could afford such unparalleled generosity, it was certainly the Bronx Bombers. They had already won 15 pennants; and despite their pitchers' largesse on September 11, they added the '49 flag, too.

The Proof Is in the Burning

After a morning workout, Giant slugger Johnny Mize came into the clubhouse dripping with perspiration. He flung off his sweatshirt and headed for the showers. While Mize was washing off, trainer Frank Bowman took Mize's sweatshirt and soaked it with alcohol.

When Mize came back to his locker, Bowman asked him how he had been feeling.

"Fine," Mize replied. "Bushed from the workout, but otherwise just fine."

"Well," said Bowman, "you'd better stay away from the hard stuff, John. That's what really takes it out of a player."

"What are you talking about, Frank? I was in before curfew last night, and all I had was a couple of beers."

"Don't try to kid me, John," the trainer said as he dropped a match onto the sweatshirt and set it aflame. "That's alcohol you sweated out!"

The embarrassed Mize rushed to quench the fire.

"Please, Doc," Mize implored, "don't say anything about this to anyone."

A Word from the Wise

In 1949, midway through a tight game between the Chicago Cubs and the Pittsburgh Pirates, Ralph Kiner stepped to the plate to face Cub hurler Bob Muncrief. The Bucs' slugger found Muncrief no mystery, as he blasted the ball against the back wall of Wrigley Field for a game-tying homer.

After retiring the side without further damage, Muncrief took his seat on the bench. Manager Frankie Frisch asked him what kind of pitch Kiner had just hit out. "A doggone good curve ball," Muncrief responded. "He hit a good pitch."

"Well, forget about your curve," Frisch advised, "and just throw him fastballs next time up. He won't even get a loud foul off you."

On Kiner's next turn, he found two teammates aboard. Muncrief threw him a fastball, and Ralph catapulted this one *over* the back wall and into orbit.

Muncrief walked back to the bench and glared at Frisch. "Well, brains," he shouted, "he hit yours a whole lot farther than he hit mine."

DURING HIS 24-year career, Beans Reardon was regarded as one of the game's more colorful arbiters. One afternoon, while he was calling the plays at third base, Richie Ashburn came sliding in under the tag of Brooklyn's Billy Cox.

"Safe," Beansie yelled—but he raised his thumb to give the "out" sign.

Ashburn exploded, but Reardon calmly disarmed him. "You heard me call you safe," Beans said. "But 30,000 people saw me call you out. So you're out."

The Yankee Clipper Comes Back

The 1949 season was near the halfway mark, and the name of Joe DiMaggio had yet to appear in a Yankee box score. During the winter, Joltin' Joe had undergone an operation to remove a painful bone spur in his right heel. He had missed all of spring training plus the first 66 games of the schedule.

The Yanks were locked in a pennant struggle with the Red Sox, who had won 10 of their last 11 games. The two teams were about to clash in a crucial series in Fenway Park. On the eve of the Yanks' departure for Boston, DiMag decided he would give it a try, and he traveled up to Beantown on his own.

When he arrived at Fenway, Joe asked manager Casey Stengel to insert him in the lineup. Casey did, figuring that even if Joe could make no tangible contribution, he would provide an inspiration to his mates.

But DiMaggio's contributions were tangible, indeed. Though he hadn't hit a pitch for eight months, Joe laced out a single on his first time up. On his second trip, he socked a homer which proved to be the key hit in a 5-4 Yank victory.

The next day, Joe hit two homers—the first was a three-run shot, and the second broke a 7-7 tie to win the game.

And in the third game of the series, Joe hit another three-run homer, this time in the seventh inning.

In the three-game series, he had hit four homers and knocked in nine runs! DiMaggio went on to bat .346 in his abbreviated season, and he led the Yanks to a pennant and a World Series championship.

IN 1950, SUNNY JIM KONSTANTY got the chance to work in 74 games with the Phillies. He won a neat 16 of them, lost 7, and pulled a bushel more out of the fire.

Konstanty had the singular honor of being the first—and thus far the only—relief pitcher ever to be named the Most Valuable Player of the Year!

Everything's Coming Up Rosens

In 1950, Al (Flip) Rosen flipped from nowhere onto the Cleveland ballclub. And in his very first year as a major-leaguer, he led the league in home runs.

Rosen's total was a resounding 37 homers—one short of the record for a rookie. And as if that didn't make him feel secure enough in the Indians' lineup, he batted in 116 runs besides.

THE AMERICAN LEAGUE story for 1950 can be summed up in four clipped words: strong hitting—weak pitching! And the Boston Red Sox sure did a lot of the hitting.

In a game against St. Louis on June 8, 1950, Boston scored 29 runs. In their next contest, they brought in 20; in the third, they scored seven; and in the fourth, they tallied eight times. In one whale of a walloping four-game series, the Red Sox stepped on home plate 64 times!

Mastering the Tools of Ignorance

In 1946, when Yogi Berra first donned a Yankee uniform, few thought he'd make the grade as a big-league backstop. There was no doubting his ability with the stick, but his gray matter, so it was said, left a lot to be desired. During the next two years, the Yanks tried him in the outfield, but Yogi made too many hearts palpitate as he circled seemingly bewildered under easy fly balls. In 1949, Casey Stengel ended that experiment and brought Yogi behind the plate to stay.

But Yogi did not immediately justify his manager's confidence. In 1950, he tied the major-league record for passed balls.

And the next year, Yogi dropped a pop foul hit by Ted Williams that would have been the final out in an Allie Reynolds no-hitter. Luckily for Yogi, however, Allie got Williams to pop the next pitch to the very same spot behind the plate, and this time Yog held on to it.

Year by year, though, Berra's work improved steadily. So much so, in fact, that between July 27, 1957, and May 10, 1959 —a span of 148 games—he did not make a single error. That was a new all-time record, and it's still on the books.

The Grand Old Man of Baseball

A kind of lump stuck in the throats of baseball players and fans when Connie Mack announced that he was leaving the dugout to the youngsters at the close of the 1950 season. When the Old Man handed the reins of the Athletics over to Jimmy Dykes, one of his favorite pupils, you knew that an era was ending. Baseball was big business now, and the sandlot feel of the game faded into the distance.

Before the turn of the century, when "Slats" McGillicuddy was just a catcher in need of a haircut, baseball was a tough racket. Players swore so loud and so hard that a lady wouldn't be seen within one mile of a ballpark. It was Connie Mack who, in great measure, brought decency to the game. By his own quiet, dignified deportment he won the respect of public and player alike.

In his 50 years as manager of the Philadelphia Athletics, Mack won nine pennants and five World Series.

Red Smith, the famous sportswriter, traveled for some time with baseball's most beloved patriarch. It was more than mere admiration that prompted Smith to write: "He could be as tough as rawhide and gentle as a mother, reasonable and obstinate beyond reason, and courtly, benevolent, and fierce. He was kind-hearted and hard-fisted, drove a close bargain, and was suckered in a hundred deals. He was generous and thoughtful and autocratic and shy and independent and completely lovable."

The Say Hey Kid

In 1951, a 19-year-old outfielder started his career in organized baseball with Minneapolis, the New York Giants' top farm club. After 35 games, the kid was hitting an unbelievable .477, and how you gonna keep a man like that down on the farm? The Giants called him up, but Willie Mays was a little reluctant to make the move to the big time. He didn't know whether he was up to major-league pitching; he was afraid he would embarrass himself.

But manager Leo Durocher insisted, told Mays he'd do fine, that he had nothing to worry about. "You're hitting .477 where you are now. Hit half that for me, and I'll be satisfied."

So Willie came. And Willie went hitless in his first three games. He was so disconsolate that he pleaded with Durocher to send him back to the farm club.

But Durocher stuck by his decision. The next day, Mays responded with a king-sized homer off Warren Spahn, no less.

But it took the kid another three games to get another hit. At last, Willie hit his stride, and then he never stopped. He went on to win Rookie-of-the-Year honors, and played in the World Series.

During the off-season, Willie received his notice from Uncle Sam, and the Giants had to get along without him in 1952 and 1953. But they really couldn't, and they fell short of the flag each year.

160

When Mays returned in 1954, he hit .345, belted out 41 homers, drove in 110 runs. Now the Giants did make it to the World Series—and this time, they won. After the season, Willie was voted the Most Valuable Player in the league.

From then on, Mays enjoyed one great season after another in New York; and when the Giants moved to the Coast, Willie starred in his San Francisco uniform. Six times he hit over 40 homers, and twice he hit over 50. In more than 20 years in a Giant uniform, the kid from Westfield, Alabama collected 3,187 hits and 646 home runs.

In mid-1972, the Giants engineered a deal which enabled Willie to return to New York to finish out his career. Though he had played almost 15 full seasons in San Francisco, the Say Hey Kid left his heart in Gotham. The Mets wanted Mays to help instruct their youngsters, and they thought Willie might provide an occasional key hit that might take them to the pennant.

In his very first game, Willie hit a homer to snap a tie and defeat the Giants.

In his first month with his new club, Mays' bat contributed mightily to six wins. And in mid-season, he won two consecutive games with a double against the Dodgers and a homer (his 650th) against the Giants.

But at the age of 42, playing in his final year, Mays was only a shadow of his former self. He played little, and pitchers were now feeding him a diet of fastballs, proof that Willie could no longer get his bat around quick enough. But he did contribute several game-winning hits in 1973, and closed out his career as he had begun it—on a pennant-winning team. His last hit came in the 11th inning of the second game of the World Series: it was a game-winning single.

A Short Story

The St. Louis fans who came to Sportsman's Park on Sunday, August 18, 1951, didn't expect much. The bill of fare was a doubleheader between the two worst clubs in the American League—the hometown Browns and the Detroit Tigers.

What the fans didn't know was that the Browns' president, Bill Veeck, had planned a little surprise. That morning, Veeck had signed a midget named Eddie Gaedel to a formal player's contract.

In the first inning of the second game, the 46-inch-tall rookie made his major-league debut as a pinch-hitter for the Browns' scheduled leadoff man. "Now batting for Saucier," the public-address announcer intoned, "number ⅛, Gaedel."

The stands exploded with laughter as the midget marched to the plate, toy bat in hand. The umpire strode to the Browns' dugout and demanded that the farce come to an end. But the manager, Zack Taylor, reached into his pocket and pulled out Gaedel's contract. The ump was left with no choice but to allow the midget to bat.

Bob Cain, the Detroit pitcher, had to aim at a strike zone only slightly larger than a postage stamp. Ball one went sailing over Gaedel's head, and so did ball two. Now Cain was beginning to laugh himself. He lobbed the next two pitches way over the Brownie's head, and little Eddie scooted down to first. He was immediately removed for a pinch-runner, and ran off the field to the cheers of thousands.

The next day, the American League president scolded Veeck, and banned all midgets from the game. Eddie Gaedel's major-league career was over. But he and Bill Veeck had given their long-suffering fans a hearty laugh.

The Shot Heard 'Round the World

As late as August 11, 1951, the Giants were trailing the Dodgers by 13½ games. The colossal Brooklyn team was a cinch to sew up the National League flag—or so everyone thought. But in the last moments of the campaign, the never-say-die Giants caught the Brooks at the wire. The two clubs finished their regular season schedule in a dead heat.

They would have to fight it out—winner of a two-out-of-three playoff to take the pennant.

The heroes of Flatbush and the Polo Grounds split in their first two meetings. Now they were locked in the third and crucial battle. It was a pitchers' duel until late in the game, but in the eighth, the Brooks knocked out Giant pitcher Sal Maglie with a cluster of three runs. The New Yorkers now lagged behind 4-1, and in the bottom of the eighth, Brooklyn hurler Don Newcombe made the Giant hitters eat right out of his hand.

Giant hopes rose slightly as the last half of the ninth began. Alvin Dark led off by ripping a single to center. Don Mueller advanced him to third with a sharp single of his own to right. But hopes sank again when Monte Irvin popped out. Some modest cheers were heard as Whitey Lockman smashed a double, driving in Dark and making the score 4-2.

The Dodgers called on Ralph Branca to relieve Newcombe and put the game on ice.

Then up stepped the Flying Scotsman, Bobby Thomson. Benched by Giant pilot Leo Durocher earlier in the season, Bobby had come back with his powerful bat to spark the New Yorkers on their epic pennant drive. Could he perform a miracle now? For nothing less than a miracle was needed.

As Ralph Branca checked with his catcher, Rube Walker, Durocher strode down from the third-base coach's box to hold a brief get-together with Thomson. "Bobby, if you ever hit one, hit one now," pleaded Leo.

Branca delivered the first pitch—a perfect strike. Then he fired again. Thomson swung, delivering the blow tagged for baseball immortality. Up, up it went, clearing the left-field barrier for a home run!

Thomson's sensational circuit-clout had driven in three runs, and copped the game and the league flag for the Giants by a 5-4 score.

Here was a great storybook ending to one of the most spine-tingling pennant finishes in the history of the big time.

DURING AN altercation, a teammate of Yogi Berra's, at a loss for logic, ended up his side of the argument by saying, "Aw, you got the ugliest mug in baseball."

Fazed not in the least, Yogi retorted, "So what! Ya don't hit a ball wit ya face, do ya?"

ON SEPTEMBER 14, 1951, Bob Nieman stepped to the plate for his first time in the big leagues. As usual, the St. Louis Browns were enmired in the second division, and had brought up their farm phenoms for a look-see.

Nieman may have been terrified on his first trip to the plate, but he got a pitch in his power zone and belted it over the wall. Evidently, the rookie outfielder enjoyed the cheers of the fans, for the next time up, he banged out another homer. No rookie has ever matched this feat.

Indian Giver

Branch Rickey had a well-earned reputation as a tough man to deal with, when it came to contract-signing time. Preacher Roe, star Dodger pitcher in the early '50s, tells this story about one of his wrangles with the old tightwad.

The Preacher demanded a sum from Mr. Rickey that the boss deemed unreasonable. In several sessions, each of the bargainers had made minor concessions, but a considerable distance still separated the two men.

After a typically unproductive talk, Rickey suggested that Roe go home and consider the Dodgers' final offer. "By the way," Rickey added, "I've got two hunting dogs I'd like you to have. I know how much you like to hunt." The Preacher took the dogs back home, and they proved to be the best dogs he had ever had.

"One day, while I was out having a good hunt," Roe reminisces, "I got to thinking that Mr. Rickey can't be too bad a fella if he'd give me such good dogs. So I went back home, signed the contract, and put it in the mail. A few hours later, those two dogs took off across the field, and I haven't seen 'em since."

How Did He Do It?

The greatest catch ever made? No matter which one you choose, you're bound to get an argument.

There's Fred Snodgrass' beauty in the final inning of the last game of the 1912 Series, after he had muffed an easy chance.

There's the time Harry Hooper stole a home run from the Giants' Larry Doyle by catching the ball as he lay in the lap of a fan in the bleachers.

There's Al Gionfriddo's grab of a DiMaggio blast to the bull-pen in the 1947 Series. There's the diving catch Ron Swoboda made of Brooks Robinson's liner in the 1969 Series—even on the replays it looked impossible. There's Willie Mays' over-the-shoulder interception of Vic Wertz's 450-foot blast in the 1954 Series.

Each of these catches has its champions, and there are many other great plays that would receive votes. But those who were in Pittsburgh's Forbes Field on a certain evening in 1951 will tell you that they saw a Giant rookie named Mays make a catch better than any you could dream of.

Pirate first-baseman Rocky Nelson, a lefthanded batter, blasted a ball to dead center, which in Forbes Field was 457 feet.

Mays immediately turned around and dashed for the wall as fast as he could go. As he hit the warning track, he looked over his shoulder and realized that the ball had been hit so hard that it was now hooking to the right.

There was no time for Mays to reach across his body and grab the ball with his glove hand, so Willie instinctively reached down with his bare hand, and plucked the ball out of the air at his knees.

As Mays returned to the dugout grinning from ear to ear, manager Leo Durocher told everyone on the bench to give their center-fielder the silent treatment.

"Hey Leo," Willie said, not dismayed in the least, "you don't have to say, 'Nice play, Willie.' I *know* that was a nice play."

Moments later, a note came down to the Giant dugout from Pittsburgh general manager Branch Rickey. "That was the finest catch I have ever seen," Rickey wrote, "and the finest catch I ever hope to see."

WHEN MONTE IRVIN came to the major leagues as a 30-year-old rookie with the New York Giants, he was, by his own admission, "way past his peak." He had been compelled to "waste" 11 years in the Negro Leagues, where one year he had batted .422, and in another, hit 41 homers. Monte had only eight years left for the Giants, and one final season for the Cubs.

Nevertheless, when Irvin got his chance to showcase his talents before all of America, he rose to the occasion. In the first game of the 1951 World Series against the Yanks, he hit three singles and a triple to lead his Giants to victory. In the second game, he got four more hits—a double and three singles. Though his team went on to lose the Series in six games, Monte stroked 11 hits in 24 times at bat, for an average of .458.

In 1973, in recognition of his accomplishments in both the Negro Leagues and the National League, Irvin was inducted into the Hall of Fame.

ON MAY 21, 1952, the game between Cincinnati and Brooklyn was over almost as soon as it began. In the very first inning, several Red pitchers paraded to the showers as 19 consecutive Dodgers reached base. Fifteen Brooklynites scored—a National League high.

The Pirate Plague

In 1952, the Pirates were far and away the worst team in baseball. By the time the season mercifully drew to a close, the Bucs had racked up a staggering 112 losses.

But while Pirate fans suffered through their worst season ever, they kept on hearing dazzling reports about the phenoms down on the farm. Two pitchers for the baby bucs of Bristol (Tennessee), Bill Bell and Ron Necciai, were tearing up the Appalachian League. Bell pitched three no-hitters, two of them back to back, and Necciai hurled a no-hitter in which he struck out all 27 men!

The Pittsburgh front office couldn't wait to get its hands on these youngsters. If Bell and Necciai were to be the Pirates' salvation, they had to be brought up now.

The results were almost predictable. Maybe the Pirates' style of playing was contagious. Bell pitched in four games for the Bucs, losing one, winning none. Necciai pitched in 12 games, winning one and losing six.

Necciai said goodbye to Pittsburgh forever, and never pitched in the majors again. Bell pitched one more game for Pittsburgh three years later, then drifted back to the minors for good.

He Shoulda Got an Oscar

Stalling for time is one of baseball's least appreciated arts. Sometimes, for example, a relief pitcher is hustled into a ticklish situation before he's had enough time to warm up properly. When this happens, a shrewd teammate will try somehow to get the reliever a few extra pitches beyond the allowable eight.

One of the best at this maneuver was Peewee Reese, star shortstop of the Dodgers. In one game, the score was close and the Dodger starter was suddenly being clobbered. Manager Charlie Dressen brought in Clyde King to put out the fire. But when

167

King arrived on the mound, he told Dressen and Reese that he wasn't warm yet, and asked Peewee to stall a bit to get him a few more pitches. Reese agreed, and returned to his shortstop position.

As soon as King had completed his allowed eight warmup pitches, Reese "got something in his eye." In seeming agony, he asked for time out, and walked over to third baseman Billy Cox for aid in removing the offending particle.

Reese's anguish seemed so sincere that King walked over to third to see if he could help!

BILLY LOES is perhaps best known for his explanation as to why he kicked a ground ball hit back to the box in the 1952 World Series. "I lost it in the sun," the Dodger pitcher revealed after the game.

But Billy once came up with an observation that deserves an equal measure of immortality. A reporter asked Loes why such a fine pitcher as himself had never won more than 14 games. "If you win 20," Loes replied, "they want you to do it every year."

They Love Me, They Love Me Not

There are two baseball men—one a player, the other a manager —who have been in and out of clubs almost more times than they can remember. An itinerary of the complicated peregrinations of each one of them would look like an F.B.I. dossier.

To start with, let's take Bobo Newsom. Newsom had already played for three clubs before joining Washington early in the 1935 season. After two years, the Senators tired of Bobo and shipped him to Fenway Park. But in 1942, the Senators began to miss him, and reacquired his contract from Detroit.

Before the 1942 season was over, Washington sent Bobo down the road again, this time to Brooklyn.

The Dodgers then traded Newsom to St. Louis. But the Browns rerouted Bobo to the nation's capital. There he pitched in only six games before again packing his bags and heading for Philadelphia.

After three years with the A's, Bobo was once again called back to duty in Griffith Stadium, where he labored two more years. In 1948, the Senators dealt him off to the Yanks.

At last, in 1952, the weary Bobo, now 45 years old, made his fifth and final stop in Washington. But the Senators showed no compassion for this senior citizen. They shipped him to Philadelphia, where he ended his career at the age of 46.

The Senators had traded *for* Newsom five times, and had traded him *away* five times. In addition, Bobo wore the uniforms of seven other clubs. St. Louis traded him three times, and Brooklyn twice.

More recently, Danny Murtaugh has had the same yo-yo relationship with Pittsburgh. From 1948 to 1951, he was the Pirate second-baseman before hanging up his spikes as a player. Six years later, however, the last-place Buccaneers called on him to replace Bobby Bragan as manager. When Danny led his team from the cellar to second in 1958 and to the flag in 1960, he was hailed as a genius.

But as the Pirates slipped to seventh place in 1961, Murtaugh was magically transformed into an ignoramus. By 1965, he was out of a job.

Danny's successor, Harry Walker, wasn't a big hit in the Steel City, and when the front office decided that Harry had to go, they rehired Murtaugh to finish out the '67 campaign.

But the managerial contract for 1968 was awarded to Larry Shepard, who lasted about as long as Walker did. So the successor to Harry was now chosen as the successor to Larry.

Murtaugh took Pittsburgh to the Eastern Division title in 1970 and 1971, and then ill health forced him to turn the helm over to one of his coaches, Bill Virdon. Bill's hold on Pirate affections withered late in the 1973 season, and Pittsburgh needed a new manager. Need we tell you whom they turned to?

ST. LOUIS BROWNS' fans couldn't be blamed if they thought they saw a conga line of Boston Red Sox dancing around the bases. In the seventh inning of a game played on June 18, 1953, the Sox scored 17 runs before Brownie pitchers could get the third out.

Boston outfielder Gene Stephens set a record in that inning by coming to the plate three times and banging out three hits. And catcher Sammy White set another record by scoring three times.

You can bet that the Browns' pitchers were singing the St. Louis Blues in that marathon seventh inning.

Bobo—a Bolt from the Blue

For a meteoric rise to fame and an equally meteoric descent to obscurity, it's hard to top the story of Alva "Bobo" Holloman. An unheralded rookie, Holloman made the St. Louis Browns' pitching staff in spring training of 1953. For the first month, he spent most of his time sitting in the bullpen, getting an occasional call for mop-up work.

On May 6, 1953, the Browns' manager gave Bobo the ball and told him he was the starting pitcher against the Philadelphia Athletics. Bobo justified his manager's confidence. He threw a no-hitter!

But from that day on, it was all downhill. Whatever had baffled the batters in Bobo's first start proved no mystery the rest of the year. Before the season was over, Bobo found himself back in the minors.

MANY PLAYERS have hit the ball a country mile, but none ever hit a ball farther than Mickey Mantle. In 1953, Mantle, a switch-hitter, came to the plate against the Senators' Chuck Stobbs. Batting lefthanded, the young Yankee slugger belted a shot over the center-field fence at Washington's Griffith Stadium. The ball was still climbing as it left the ballpark, and landed 565 feet away from home plate, the longest homer ever measured.

UMPIRE AUGIE DONATELLI once threw Giant great Bobby Thomson out of a ballgame. Years later, Thomson—a quiet, well-behaved chap—told the arbiter that he was the only umpire ever to give him the thumb.

"My honor was at stake," Augie explained. "I called a strike on you, and you called me a bad name."

"Yes, I did," the Flying Scot agreed. "But why did you kick me out? Only you, me, and the catcher heard it."

"I know," Augie said, "but I didn't want that catcher to go through life thinking that's what I am!"

Necessity Is the Mother of Invention

In 1954, the Milwaukee Braves went into spring training brimming with optimism. While the hot-stove league was in session, they had pulled off a big trade with the Giants that had brought them Bobby Thomson. The New York veteran, the front-office people figured, would complement the Braves' young star, Eddie Mathews who, in 1953, had blossomed with 47 homers.

But when Thomson broke a leg during an exhibition game, 1954 suddenly looked like a terrible year. Who would play the outfield spot that had been staked out for Thomson? But then manager Charley Grimm rememberd that a 20-year-old second-baseman had hit a long homer the day before Thomson's mishap.

"Try the outfield," he told the rookie, who hadn't been too nimble around second. The kid tried the outfield, and he played there for the next two decades.

The kid's name? Henry Aaron, of course.

LATE IN THE 1936 season, the Cardinals reached down into the minor leagues and brought up a 24-year-old first-baseman named Walter Alston. The kid cracked the lineup for only a few innings in one game, and struck out in his only at-bat. He never dented another big-league box score.

But in 1954, Smokey Alston reappeared on the scene as the

manager of the Dodgers. Twenty years later, he still held that post. The obscure first-baseman had become the dean of major-league managers, and had led his Dodgers to seven pennants and four World Series championships.

QUITE A FEW players have managed to belt four homers in one game, though, interestingly enough, neither Babe Ruth nor Hank Aaron ever turned the trick. What made Joe Adcock's four homers against Brooklyn on July 31, 1954, so memorable was the double he added. That fifth hit gave him a total of 18 bases for the day —a slugging achievement no one has ever matched.

Fluttering Off to the Funny Farm

In the eighth inning of a game on September 10, 1954, Giant backstop Ray Katt looked like a man trying to catch a butterfly without a net. Katt was trying, without much success, to hold on to the knuckleballs served up by Hoyt Wilhelm. Before the inning was over, the poor backstop was charged with four passed balls, a major-league record.

But Wilhelm didn't play favorites when it came to embarrassing his battery mates. In 1958, Old Sarge moved on to Baltimore, and soon went to work on Oriole catchers Gus Triandos, Charlie Lau, and Joe Ginsberg. In different games, each man suffered the indignity of watching three pitches sail by—an American League record.

Trusty Dusty

In 1954, the Cleveland Indians rolled to the pennant while winning 111 games, an American League record. Over in the National League, New York had been rejuvenated by the return of Willie Mays from the Army, and beat out the Dodgers for the flag. Though the Giants were a fine team, they figured to be patsies for the Indian steamroller.

But as often happens in postseason play, things do not work

out the way they figure to. The Giants went on to sweep the Indians in four straight games, thanks largely to the efforts of a pinch-hitter named Dusty Rhodes.

In the first game, Dusty came up in the tenth inning with two men on and the score tied, 2-2. He resolved the deadlock immediately by clouting the first pitch for a homer.

In the second game, the Giants called on his services a little earlier. It was the fifth inning, and they trailed 1-0. With two men out, Rhodes laced a single to tie the game, and the Giants scored one more to take the lead. To keep his hot bat in the lineup, Rhodes was inserted into left field. When he came up again in the seventh, he belted a homer to give the Giants an all-important insurance run.

Giant manager Leo Durocher now knew he had lightning in a bottle, and when the Giants loaded the bases in the third inning of the third game, he did not hesitate. He called on Dusty again. The pinch-hitter *par excellence* delivered a single, and the Giants had two runs on their way to a 6-2 win.

In the fourth and final game, Dusty's talents were not needed as the Giants jumped out to an early 7-0 lead, which stood up to gain the victory.

The Giants had pulled the World Series upset of the decade, led by a man who was not good enough to make their starting lineup. In six at-bats, Dusty Rhodes had come up with four hits —two of them for the full distance. The incredible pinch-hitter had driven in seven runs!

Next Year Comes at Last

"The Brooks are jinxed!" everybody was saying as the seventh and deciding game of the 1955 World Series got under way. Five times before, Dodger pennant-winners had met the high-flying Yankees in Series play—and five times Brooklyn had gone down to bitter defeat. "Wait 'til next year" became the motto of the ever faithful Dodger rooters.

Though the fans still refused to give up, the experts were laying odds on the Yankees to wrap up the 1955 championship—

especially since the final game was being played on the New Yorkers' home grounds.

When Dodger Manager Walt Alston called on pitcher Johnny Podres to carry the load on the crucial day of October 4, the oldtimers shook their heads in disbelief. Sure, Johnny had won the third game of the Series for the Brooks only a few days before. But now the Dodgers were in too tight a spot to depend on a 23-year-old kid.

Against young Podres, who had lost more games than he'd won during the regular season, canny Yankee manager Casey Stengel sent his veteran hurler, Tommy Byrne. Casey had led the Bombers to five straight World Series triumphs, and he had every intention of making it six. He knew that steady Tommy would be ice-cold when it counted—but would Podres crack under the terrific pressure?

Podres got into trouble early in the game, when hard-hitting Yogi Berra led off the fourth inning by dropping a double into left-center. But Berra died on base as Johnny bore down. When the Brooks got to Byrne for two hard-earned runs, Dodger rooters began to dream of the impossible—a World Series crown, the first in the long history of the valiant Ebbets Fielders.

But the Yankees hadn't given up yet! In the bottom half of the sixth, Yankee runners reached second and third with none out. The Bombers threatened to break the game wide open. Plucky Podres, helped by a magnificent catch by little left-fielder Sandy Amoros, pitched his way out of hot water.

In the eighth, New York's powerful bats spoke loudly again. With only one out, the tying Yankee runs were on first and third. Cool and collected, as if he had made a habit of mowing down fearsome Yankee sluggers all his life, Podres retired the side.

Not a single run could be scored against Johnny. It was his day, and the greatest day in the annals of Dodgerdom. When the last Yankee had succumbed to Podres' masterful pitching in the ninth, a tremendous roar from more than 60,000 throats shook the vast confines of Yankee Stadium. The mighty Yankees had been beaten, shut out by young Podres in their own backyard!

After seven fruitless and heartbreaking attempts, the Dodgers had finally won a World's Championship. No wonder there was dancing in the streets of Brooklyn! No wonder that Brooklyn fans went completely wild! And no wonder that Johnny Podres will never be forgotten, for he gave one of the greatest exhibitions of clutch pitching in the history of the game.

THE 1955 ALL-STAR game was in the bottom of the twelfth inning, all tied up at 5 and 5. As Stan Musial stepped in the batter's box, American League catcher Yogi Berra moaned, "Boy, my feet are killing me."

"Relax," soothed Stan the Man. "I'll have you home in a minute." He then hit the first pitch thrown to him for a game-breaking homer.

GENERAL MANAGER Hank Greenberg once received an unsigned contract from one of his Cleveland players. He immediately sent a telegram to the disgruntled employee: "In your haste to accept the terms, you forgot to sign the contract."

The next day, Greenberg got a wire from the player, reading: "In your haste to give me a raise, you put in the wrong figure."

A Homer a Day Keeps the Boo Birds at Bay

In 1955, in his first season as the regular first-baseman for the Pirates, Dale Long hit a very respectable .291, and also managed to connect with an occasional homer.

But no one was prepared for Dale's long-ball rampage in May of 1956. The 30-year-old first-sacker hit a homer a game *for eight consecutive games!*

ROBIN ROBERTS was no slouch on the mound. For six straight years, he notched 20 or more wins for the Philadelphia Phils. But successful as he was, the fastballing righthander always had a penchant for delivering gopher balls.

When Roberts finally missed the 20-game circle in 1956, the batters really teed off on him. Though he managed to win 19 games, he gave up a record 46 four-baggers.

ON SEPTEMBER 21, 1956, the Yankees left 20 juicy runs dangling on the bases, never to be scored.

It seems incredible that a team should have an average of more than two men an inning left on the bases for an entire nine-inning game. Yet Yankee fans can only read the numbers and weep!

A Day to Remember

It's Brooklyn against New York in the Series.

Sal Maglie pitched the opener and won. He gave up nine hits. Don Larsen started the second game for the Yanks, but the Brooks raked him for four runs and he was sent to the showers during the second inning.

Now in this fifth game of the Series, it's Maglie versus Larsen. Neither of these pitchers showed up too well in his first start.

But this is another afternoon and a new game. During the first four innings, Don retired the Dodgers in one-two-three order. Sure, he looked much better than in his earlier outing. But what of it? Pitchers have been known to pitch perfect ball for a few frames and then blow sky-high.

The fifth inning is on and Gil Hodges connects. A screaming drive whistles into left-center. It looks like the first hit for the

Dodgers. But out of nowhere charges Mickey Mantle to make an extraordinary catch.

Now Sandy Amoros is up. He leans into a pitch and sends it rocketing toward the right-field stands. It looks like a home run. At the last second, the ball curves foul.

The sixth and seventh innings pass. Still no hits, no walks, no nothing for the Dodgers. The crowd is quiet as Larsen goes through his no-windup deliveries. Then Yankee Stadium is rocked with a big roar as he retires another batter.

Now it's the eighth. Again Hodges is at bat. This time, he lines a sizzling drive to the left of third baseman Andy Carey. The Yankee infielder lunges to his left and comes up with a brilliant putout.

More cheers; more labored breathing; more fingernail biting. And now it's the ninth! The Yanks lead 2-0. *Only three more batters,* and Larsen will have the first no-hitter—the first perfect game—in Series history!

Carl Furillo lifts an easy fly to right field and Bauer gobbles it up. Roy Campanella slaps a grounder at second baseman Billy Martin. Billy's fielding is sure, his throw is swift and accurate. There are *two* outs.

Maglie is due up next. The pinch-hitter is Dale Mitchell. He's a tough man—hits to all fields, rarely strikes out. Is it going to end here?

Larsen bears down harder on each pitch. He pitches a ball. Then a strike. Then another strike! Mitchell fouls off the next serve. Now Larsen rears back and puts everything he has on a fastball. Mitchell lets it go by. Up goes the right hand of plate umpire Babe Pinelli.

It's all over! The impossible has happened! Twenty-seven Brooklyn batters have gone to the plate, and 27 have sat right down again. The first no-hitter—and the first perfect game—in Series play is in the books.

ST. PETERSBURG, FLORIDA, where the Yankees customarily reside during spring training, is well known as a haven for pensioners. One spring, after his perfect game in the World Series,

pitcher Don Larsen made the local papers by wrapping his new car around a lamppost at 5 A.M. Yankee manager Casey Stengel was asked if he planned to fine Larsen.

"Anybody who can find something to do in St. Petersburg at five in the morning," Casey quipped, "deserves a medal, not a fine."

Lew Comes Through

"Look Lew," said Manager Fred Haney after the Braves had lost the sixth game of the 1957 World Series. "Spahn is down with the flu. He's too weak to pitch. I'm counting on you. I know you've only had two days rest, but you're the best I have."

Haney knew what he was talking about. Burdette had won the second game, 4-2, to tie the Series. Then he shut out the Yanks, 1-0, in the fifth contest to give Milwaukee a 3-2 edge. He had blanked the Bombers for 15 straight innings.

Many observers felt that Haney was stretching his luck. Burdette couldn't continue his streak. The Yanks were sure-fire bets to take him apart.

Opposing Burdette was Don Larsen, the hero of the 1956 World Series.

When Stengel announced before game time that the mighty Mickey Mantle, who had been out with injuries, would be back in action in the final fracas, things looked serious for Burdette and the Braves.

And when Hank Bauer opened the first inning by hitting Burdette's very first pitch for a double, things looked downright glum.

But right then and there, the big righthander settled down. He retired the next three batters in apple-pie order.

In the third frame, the Braves let loose with a four-run barrage that shelled Larsen from the box. Now Burdette had a margin to work with. But could he keep that lead?

The Yanks got another man on base when Jerry Coleman singled in the fifth. But Burdette again held New York at bay, and stretched his scoreless-inning streak to 20.

When Del Crandall unloaded a homer in the eighth, the score became Milwaukee 5, New York 0.

Then the last half of the ninth. The 60,000 fans grew tense as the Bomber bats were arrayed for a last stand. The first Yank up was retired. Now Burdette and the gallant Milwaukee Braves needed only two more outs to win their first World's Championship.

But Gil McDougald singled; and although Tony Kubek was counted as the second out, Coleman outlegged an infield hit, and Tommy Byrne got another.

The bases were loaded! Burdette was tiring. The Yankee fans were agog as their big rally seemed to take shape. Yankee luck! Yankee pluck! Would it pull them through at the very last minute as it had so many times in the past?

All eyes turned to the long, lank figure in the pitcher's box. Burdette delivered. Moose Skowron connected, banging a sharp grounder down the third-base line. It looked like a sure double! But Ed Mathews, his back to the ball, scooped it up and stepped on third to end the game.

Burdette had completed one of the most outstanding exhibitions of sustained pitching mastery of all time. He had blanked the Yanks for 24 consecutive innings, and in the process had given Milwaukee its first World's Championship.

Pilots of the Bronx Bombers

What makes a great manager? Whatever it is, both Joseph V. McCarthy and Charles Dillon Stengel had it. Each piloted the New York Yankees to seven World Series championships, an all-time baseball record.

Joe's first champs were the 1932 Yankees. He won Series honors again in 1936, 1937, 1938, 1939, 1941, and 1943. Marse Joe also led two other pennant winners—the 1929 Cubs and the Yanks of 1942.

Casey's first five years as helmsman of the Bronx Bombers —1949 to 1953—brought five World's Championships. He added two other titles in 1956 and 1958. In all, Casey took his team to the Series ten times—more than anyone else.

IT WASN'T Elroy Face's fault that the Pittsburgh Pirates didn't win the pennant in 1959. Of the 58 relief appearances the little forkball artist made that year, he won 18 and lost only one. He was the winner in his first 17 decisions before finally losing a game.

And his winning percentage—.947—is the highest ever.

The Toughest Loss

On the night of May 29, 1959, lefthander Harvey Haddix took the mound for the Pittsburgh Pirates against the hometown Milwaukee Braves. Inning after inning, he set down the side in order while his opponent, Lew Burdette, struggled to keep Pirate runners from reaching the plate. At the end of the regulation nine innings, Haddix had joined baseball's immortals by retiring all 27 batters who faced him.

Only seven men had pitched a perfect game before him, only five in the modern era. Unfortunately for Haddix, however, his teammates had been unable to score off Burdette, though they had scratched out several hits.

The game wore on through the tenth, eleventh, and twelfth innings without score, and Haddix's perfect game remained unblemished.

In the thirteenth, the Braves' first batter hit a routine grounder to third which Pirate Don Hoak bobbled. Now the perfect game was over, though Haddix still had a no-hitter going. The next batter sacrificed.

With a man on second and Henry Aaron at the plate, Haddix decided that discretion would be the better part of valor, and intentionally walked the slugger. But the next man up was Joe Adcock, a doughty batsman in his own right, and Adcock slammed the ball over the fence.

Haddix had retired 36 batters in a row, more than any other pitcher ever has in one game, yet left the mound a loser. For 12 innings, he had pitched perfect ball, but perfection was not enough.

CHUCK ESSEGIAN was a star football player at Stanford, and played in the 1952 Rose Bowl. But his first love was baseball; and he had to toil long in the minors before getting his first big-league shot with the Phils in 1958.

After a brief stay in St. Louis the next year, Essegian was picked up by the Dodgers to supply some right-handed power on the bench. He did just that, batting .304 and helping L.A. to win

the flag. And in the Series, Chuck belted two pinch homers—the first man ever to do so—and led his club to the championship.

Though Essegian never again scaled such heights, he is one of only a handful of men who can look back on their achievements in the classic of college football and the pinnacle of professional baseball.

The Rookie Steals the Spotlight

The scoreboard told the tale: "Dodgers 8, White Sox 0." The crowd of 48,000 assembled in Comiskey Park sat back, hushed and just about resigned to a horrendous shellacking of their heroes.

It was the last of the fourth inning. Johnny Podres, Los Angeles southpaw, was mowing down the Sox batters.

One Sox batter had bitten the dust when Jim Landis got to first by being struck with a pitched ball. Then Sherm Lollar walked, putting Chicago runners on first and second. Up strode mighty Ted Kluszewski, a muscleman who had already belted out two homers in the Series. The spectators suddenly woke up. "Go, Go, Go," they shouted.

There was a sharp crack as Big Klu connected. The ball streaked like a meteor—400 feet up into the right-field stands. The White Sox had narrowed the gap to 8 to 3.

Visibly shaken, pitcher Podres handed Al Smith a base on balls. Dodger Manager Walter Alston took this as his signal to leap from the dugout. He had a few words with Podres, then signaled the bullpen.

No one had to be told who the new pitcher was. Alston was going with his best. He *had* to. The Dodgers needed but a single victory to wrap up the first World's Championship for Los Angeles. And the player who had done an awful lot to prepare this prize package was now approaching the pitcher's mound. His name was Larry Sherry.

This was the unknown who had come up to L.A. from the minors late in June—the kid who had gone on to spark the Dodgers to a pennant.

Then came the Series. The Dodgers were up against a speedy, aggressive team with loads of talent. The "Go-Go" Sox showed their class in the first game, blanking L.A. 11 to 0.

In the second game, after the Dodgers took a 4-2 lead in the seventh, Manager Alston entrusted Sherry with the chips-are-down chore. Larry came through, yielding only a single run in the final three innings.

With the Dodgers ahead 2-0 in the eighth inning of the third game, pitcher Drysdale lost his stuff. He had given up one run and the Sox had a couple of runners on the bases, when in strolled fireman Sherry to douse the Sox rally under a deluge of curves and fastballs.

The following day, Sherry was again the hero. With the score knotted at 4-4 in the eighth, he relieved Roger Craig, and Sherry set Chicago on its ear. In the Los Angeles half, Hodges homered, and Sherry protected the advantage. The Series stood Los Angeles 3, Chicago 1.

However, the White Sox bounced back to take the fifth in a tight 1-0 struggle.

Now in the sixth game, Sherry was once again taking the long march in from the bullpen.

While Al Smith did a tantalizing dance off first base, Bubba Phillips, the next Chicago hitter, greeted Sherry with a sharp single. Jim McAnany struck out. But Earl Torgeson, a pinch-hitter, walked. *Two down. The bases filled.* Luis Aparicio, always dangerous, was at the plate. Larry was in deep trouble. He bore down. He nailed Aparicio on a pop fly.

That was Chicago's last threat. Sherry set the remaining batters down like tenpins, hurling shutout ball for the next five innings, chalking up his second triumph of the Series.

The Dodgers had brought the World's Championship to Los Angeles. And the toast of California was Larry Sherry, who less than four months earlier, had yet to appear in his first big-league ballgame!

The Bat Is Mightier Than the Pen

Journeyman pitcher Pedro Ramos admitted that his greatest ambition when he came to the major leagues in 1955 was to strike out Ted Williams. When after five years the righthander finally accomplished the feat, he saved the ball and asked Williams to autograph it.

The next time Ramos faced Williams, the Bosox thumper clouted one of his serves for a tape-measure home run. As Williams trotted around the bases, he called out to the hurler, "Get that one back and I'll autograph it, too."

THE 1960 SEASON was not far under way when Cubs' owner Phil Wrigley decided that he would not sit back and watch his team fail to crack .500 for the fifteenth straight year. In desperation, he fired manager Charlie Grimm, and replaced him with the team's radio announcer, Lou Boudreau. This worked so well that the Cubs won 14 fewer games than they had the year before.

In 1961, Wrigley dismissed Boudreau and hired—no one. Forsaking the traditional practice of having only one man give the orders, Wrigley installed a rotating staff of coaches to guide his aimless Cubbies. The team was now so befuddled that it won six less games than it did in 1960.

In 1962, Wrigley persevered. He would stick by his new system, come hell or high water. And both came, as the Cubs won one game less than they did in 1961. Only the first-year Mets kept the Cubs from dropping out of the bottom of the league.

In 1963, Wrigley abandoned his pet project. The Cub players were mightily relieved, and the team finished two games over .500, the best mark achieved in Chicago since 1946.

IT WAS MID-SEASON, 1960, and neither the Detroit Tigers nor the Cleveland Indians were going anywhere. Following traditional front-office policy, each club figured it was time to fire the manager. While Detroit cut loose Jimmie Dykes, Cleveland dismissed Joe Gordon. Dykes was immediately signed to pilot the Indians, and Gordon took over the Tiger helm.

The bizarre managerial shift made good copy on the sports pages, but it did little to help either ballclub. Both Cleveland and Detroit finished under .500.

As Time Goes By

In 1960, the Chicago White Sox brought up a bonus baby from the Deep South for some big-league exposure. Sox manager Al Lopez had the kid sit beside him on the bench in order to absorb a few of the subtleties of the game.

One afternoon, Nellie Fox opened the second inning by

drawing a walk. When the next batter lined a hit down the right-field line, Nellie rounded second and raced for third, but a perfect throw by outfielder Roger Maris cut him down.

"He was right to try for third," Lopez told the kid. "You won't see another throw like that in a hundred years."

In the seventh inning, with Fox again on first, the same batter lined a hit to the same spot, and the same Roger Maris cut down Fox at third.

"Mister Lopez," the Southern rookie dryly drawled, "time sure does fly by here in the North."

Bowing Out in Style

It was a cold Wednesday afternoon in Boston when Ted Williams took the field for the last time. The crowd was barely over 10,000, though in succeeding years the number of people who claim to have been in Fenway Park that day has swelled to ten times that number.

Williams was concluding a great comeback year. In 1959, the year before, aches and pains had driven his batting average down to .254, the only time Ted had dipped below .300 since he broke in with the Sox in 1939. But his determination to go out of baseball as he had come in—a great hitter—was rewarded with a .316 average in 1960.

On this September 26, the Red Sox were facing Baltimore. In the first inning, Orioles' starter Steve Barber was wild, and walked Williams on four pitches. When Ted came up again in the third, Jack Fisher had replaced Barber on the mound. Ted took a big cut and flied deep to center. He was letting it all out now in an attempt to send one last ball soaring downtown.

In the fifth, the ball cracked off Ted's bat and rocketed out to right. Oriole right-fielder Al Pilarcik went back to the wall and just stood there, with his hands at his sides, as the ball sailed toward the bullpen. But the gusty September wind of Fenway held the ball up at the fence, and it dropped almost straight down into Pilarcik's waiting glove.

One more chance. In the eighth, Williams faced Fisher again, and this time he smacked the ball so hard that no wind could keep it in the park.

In his final at-bat, Ted Williams had hit his final homer—number 521 of a fantastic career.

IN 1960, LEO DUROCHER was one of the speakers at a baseball banquet. He regaled the audience with tales about the great Willie Mays—how he could hit, run, throw, and field better than just about anyone who had ever played the game.

When the Lip sat down, Lefty O'Doul stood up and asked whether Durocher had forgotten men named Ruth, Wagner, Speaker, and Cobb. Mays was a great fielder, O'Doul said, and he could run bases with the best, but he sure couldn't hit with the likes of Cobb.

When O'Doul had finished saying his piece, someone in the audience asked him what he thought Cobb would hit today, with the lively ball and the ban on trick pitches like the spitter.

"About the same as Mays," Lefty replied, "maybe .340."

"Then why do you say Cobb was so great, if he could only hit .340 with the lively ball today?"

"Well," O'Doul said, "you have to take into consideration that the man is now 73 years old."

A Grand Finale to a Grand Series

The place was Pittsburgh's Forbes Field; the date, October 13, 1960. It was late afternoon on a hazy autumn day. Not an ordinary day, this, but the seventh and deciding game of the most exciting World Series in years.

It was the ninth inning, and there were a lot of nines floating about in the knotted atmosphere. The score was 9-9, tied up as tight as an overseas Christmas parcel.

The first Buc batter strolled to the plate. He was Bill Mazeroski, clutching his warclub like Mighty Casey of old. This was the fateful moment. A hush fell upon the stands.

Ralph Terry's first pitch was a ball. But Mazeroski swung at the second. The ball soared toward the wall in left-center as Berra and Mantle raced toward it. Up and up and up wafted the ball until it sailed over the wall at the 402-foot mark—out of sight!

The 36,683 fans in the park swarmed deliriously over the field; but the echo of that mighty blow reverberated through the entire city of Pittsburgh. The town was struck with the kind of noisy madness that can only seize a major-league city that hasn't won a World's Championship for 35 years.

The 1960 World Series was dramatic all the way. The first game was won by the Pirates; the second by the Yanks. Then Pittsburgh took a 3-2 lead; but New York squared it all with a crushing 12-0 victory behind lefty Whitey Ford.

The deciding game was a nerve-tingling struggle. Pittsburgh ran off to a 4-0 lead in the first two innings. The Bucs walloped Bob Turley and pummeled his successor, Bill Stafford.

Stengel's Yanks scored a solitary marker in the fifth. But in the sixth, the Bombers suddenly opened fire on Vernon Law, and on relief ace Elroy Face. They scored four times, tallying three runs on Yogi Berra's homer. It looked like the Yanks would do it again.

They were now in the lead, 5-4, and the Yankees seldom slipped when ahead. When New York added two more tallies off Face in the eighth for a 7-4 advantage, it seemed that Stengel, the Yank's wily Ol' Perfesser, had his eighth World Series all wrapped up.

But in the last of the eighth, the never-say-die Pirates erupted for five runs. When Hal Smith belted an electrifying homer to score three runs, Pittsburgh went as crazy as a quilt. Danny Murtaugh's Bucs had turned the tables—they were now in front 9-7.

In the top of the ninth, the Yanks bounced back and counted twice as they routed Bob Friend. Bobby Richardson opened with a single. Pinch-hitter Dale Long followed with another one-bagger, sending Richardson to second. Southpaw Harvey Haddix relieved. Haddix got Roger Maris to foul out to catcher Hal Smith. But the great Mickey Mantle singled to right, scoring Richardson and moving Long to third. At this juncture, Gil McDougald was sent in to run for Long.

Now the dangerous Berra approached the plate. The tying and winning runs were on the basepaths. Yogi grounded sharply down the first-base line. Rocky Nelson grabbed the ball, stepped on the bag for one out, but he had no play at second on Mantle.

Meanwhile, McDougald crossed the plate with the equalizing tally! When the Pirates came to bat, the score was 9-9 as Mazeroski approached the plate. Two minutes later, the big Series was a matter of history.

The Age of Expansion
1961-1976

In 1957, when the Dodgers moved to Los Angeles and the Giants came to San Francisco, the national pastime at last reached nationwide. Both teams struck gold in the baseball-hungry West, with fat attendance figures and lucrative television contracts.

Not surprisingly, the American League decided that it, too, wanted a piece of the action. So in 1961, the Americans expanded their circuit to 10 teams, placing one franchise in Los Angeles and another in Washington (which the Senators had just vacated in favor of Minneapolis-St. Paul).

In 1962, the National League added two teams of its own: the Mets in New York, and the Colt .45's—later to become the Astros—in Houston. This initial foray into the South was followed up four years later by the Milwaukee Braves, who headed for Atlanta.

Also in 1966, in a less ambitious journey, the Angels moved from Los Angeles to Anaheim.

Two years later, the A's left Kansas City for greener pastures in Oakland.

All this shifting around indicated that baseball still had untapped markets; so in 1969, each league added two more teams: Montreal and San Diego in the National League, and Kansas City and Seattle in the American. Now each circuit was divided into two divisions of six teams each.

But the wanderlust of the baseball owners was still not sated. In the next five years, the Seattle Pilots became the Milwaukee Brewers, the Washington Senators became the Texas Rangers, and the San Diego Padres threatened to become the third team to be called the Washington Senators.

Where will major-league baseball go next? Honolulu? Toronto? Mexico City? Tokyo? No place on the globe is out of the question. Before the '70s are over, the Great American Game could well spread across the Pacific.

Chasing the Ghost of the Babe

In 1961, Yankee teammates Roger Maris and Mickey Mantle were conducting a double-barreled assault on one of baseball's greatest records—Babe Ruth's 60 homers in a single season. After 134 games, Maris had hit 53 round-trippers, four more than Ruth had collected at that point in 1927. Mantle had clouted only 48.

But the home-run challenge was complicated by the fact that, due to expansion of the American League in 1961, the schedule called for 162 games—eight more than were played in 1927. Commissioner Ford Frick ruled that if Ruth's name were to be taken from the record books, Maris or Mantle would have to surpass 60 homers within 154 games.

As September wore on, Mantle faded from the race, but Maris doggedly hung in. However, the extraordinary pressure of Roger's season-long pursuit of Ruth was taking its toll. Newsmen swarmed around Maris every moment of the day, and he was becoming so tense that his hair was beginning to fall out. As Roger came into game 154, he needed two homers to catch the Babe. He hit only one.

At last, in game 160, he swatted number 60. When he failed to add a homer the next day, he was left with one last chance. Midway through the final game, Red Sox pitcher Tracy Stallard served one up into Maris' power alley, and it was gone. Yankee Stadium erupted with prolonged cheers. Maris had now hit more homers in a season than anyone, but he had not dislodged Babe Ruth from the record books. For this, the fans were grateful.

Indeed, so many fans resented Maris' intrusion into Ruth's sacred realm that they never forgave him for his great year. For the rest of his stay with the Yanks, Maris heard boos every time he came to the plate. Though he played seven more years in the major leagues, he never again approached the home-run record— Ruth's or his own.

Nothing for Free

If you look at Bill Fischer's hurling record for the 1961 season, you'll find nothing remarkable either way; four games won, two games lost, while pitching for two clubs, Kansas City and Detroit.

But in 1961, Bill Fischer managed to break one of the most hallowed of all pitching records. He went 84⅓ consecutive innings *without giving up a single walk*! In so doing, he surpassed the previous record of Christy Mathewson by 16 innings.

Perfect at the Plate

Pitchers are such poor hitters that if one tops the .200 mark he becomes, in the lexicon of baseball, "a threat at the plate." But no matter how helpless a pitcher is with a bat in his hand, he can hardly help getting a few hits over the course of a season if he just keeps swinging. The law of averages, you would think, would dictate that one of these swings would drive the ball through or over the infield.

But Bob Buhl of the Milwaukee Braves was so thoroughly lousy as a batsman that for him the law of averages was repealed. In 1962, Buhl had 70 official at bats, a tally which did not include bunts or walks, yet he never lifted his batting average above .000.

IN 1962, AT THE conclusion of the New York Mets' first spring-training camp, Casey Stengel called in the press and announced his starting outfield—Frank Thomas in left, Richie Ashburn in center, and Gus Bell in right. One reporter pointed out that Thomas had six children, Ashburn six, and Bell eight.

"Well," Stengel responded, "if they produce as well on the field as they do off the field, we'll win the pennant."

Marvelous Marv

There has never been a worse club than the New York Mets of 1962. That collection of retreads, castoffs, and kids managed to win but 40 games while losing 120. What made the team so achingly awful, however, was not the number of games they lost, but the way they lost them. One of their most crushing defeats, for example, was a 15-inning game with the Phillies in which lefthander Al Jackson went all the way, allowed only three hits, and lost the game on two errors in the 15th by his first-baseman, Marv Throneberry.

When Marv's birthday rolled around later that season, center-fielder Richie Ashburn walked over to Throneberry's locker with best wishes. "We were going to give you a cake, Marv," Ashburn said, "but we thought you'd drop it."

Marvelous Marv stories are legion among Met diehards. His cast-iron hands were abetted by his leaden feet. There was the time he booted a grounder in the first inning of a game in New York to allow an unearned run. He came to bat in the bottom of the inning, and to redeem himself, walloped a mammoth drive to the deepest part of the old Polo Grounds. As the ball rolled to the wall, Marv rounded first, steamed by second, and then made a brilliant slide into third for a triple. The crowd was going wild with joy.

But the opposing team claimed that Marv had failed to touch second base, and the umpire agreed. Throneberry was called out. Met manager Casey Stengel came out of the dugout to give the arbiter what for. But before he got in so much as a word to the ump, the Mets' first-base coach said, "Don't bother, Casey. He didn't touch first either."

RIGHTHANDER TOM CHENEY pitched for three clubs in his eight-year major-league career, but he never succeeded in compiling a decent record. In no season did he win more than eight games, and in no season did he even win more games than he lost.

Yet on one September evening in 1962, Tom Cheney, hurling for the Senators, struck out more men than anyone ever has. Pitching against the Orioles, he fanned 21 men by the time his teammates got him the winning run in the bottom of the 16th inning.

Summer Re-run

The 1962 National League race ended in a dead heat between the Los Angeles Dodgers and the San Francisco Giants. As the teams squared off in a two-out-of-three playoff, the specter of

1951 loomed over the proceedings. In that year, the Giants had defeated the Dodgers in the playoff on Bobby Thomson's "shot heard 'round the world."

Just as in 1951, the Giants of 1962 won the first game and the Dodgers won the second. And just as in 1951, the Dodgers carried a big lead into the ninth inning of the final game. And again just as in 1951, the Dodgers lost the lead, and with it the pennant.

And just as in 1951, the Giants went on to lose the World Series.

ONE EVENING in late 1963, the San Francisco Giants were in New York to face the Mets at Shea Stadium. When the Giants took the field in the bottom of the first, their outfield consisted of Alou, Alou, and Alou—brothers Matty, Felipe, and Jesus. Never before had three brothers played together for one ballclub in the same game.

The novelty of this occurrence was compounded later in the game when The Brothers Alou came to bat in succession. It would have been truly heroic had they each knocked out homers, or at least base hits. But the three Alous came up, and the three Alous went down—one, two, three!

27 Up, 27 Down

The early New York Mets' fans were undoubtedly the most enthusiastic in major-league baseball. When a home-team favorite hit as much as a long fly, the noise in the Polo Grounds—or later in Shea Stadium—was deafening.

But on June 21, 1964, the New York fans were cheering for a player who was not a member of the Mets—Jim Bunning.

It took about seven innings for Met supporters to move into Bunning's corner. By that time, everyone realized that the veteran—who in his younger days had hurled a no-hitter in the American League—was on the threshold of a pitching masterpiece. He had retired the first 21 New York batters in succession. He needed only six more outs to achieve the first perfect regular-season major-league game in 42 years, the first in the National League in 84 years. If Bunning could come through, it would be the first perfect game since Don Larsen of the Yanks turned the trick in the World Series of 1956.

Only three Mets had come close to getting a hit. In the fifth inning, catcher Jesse Gonder had nearly broken up Bunning's perfect game with a hard shot toward right field. But with a diving stab at the hard-hit ball, second-baseman Tony Taylor had slapped it to the ground, and then quickly recovered it, to toss out Gonder easily.

Somewhat earlier, in the third inning, Amado Samuel had lined a ball over shortstop, but Cookie Rojas had jumped about three feet in the air to snare the pellet. A nice play.

Now, as the perfect game seemed within his grasp, the 32-year-old Bunning seemed to bear down harder. In the eighth inning, Jim struck out Joe Christopher. Gonder grounded out to second. Although Hawk Taylor struck out, he had to be thrown out at first by catcher Triandos, who dropped the third strike.

No question but that the game was in the bag for the Phillies, who were leading 6-0. The important thing now was whether righthander Bunning would tire under the pressure and in the 91-degree heat.

In the ninth, the first batter to face him, Charlie Smith, popped to Rojas in foul territory. Then George Altman, pinch-hitting for Amado Samuel, struck out.

Now the final Met batter was John Stephenson, a rookie pinch-hitting for pitcher Tom Sturdivant. When Bunning whiffed Stephenson, the entire population of Shea Stadium stood up in a rousing ovation that lasted several minutes.

Bunning had not only pitched a perfect game; he had also become the only man besides Cy Young to throw a no-hitter in each league.

THE NEW YORK YANKEES did not win their first pennant until they had been in the American League for 18 years, but did they ever make up for lost time! Since 1921, when Babe Ruth led them to that first flag, the Bronx Bombers have gone on to win 28 more. The team with the next most pennants is the Giants, who have won 14—less than half as many as the Yanks.

The Murderers' Row bunch captured seven flags. The great teams of the late '30s and '40s, led by Joe DiMaggio, won eight flags, seven of them in eight years.

But the greatest stretch of Yankee success began in 1949, when Casey Stengel arrived on the scene as manager. The awesome trio of Mantle, Berra, and Ford won 14 pennants in 16 years.

The Flag No One Wanted to Win

The Philadelphia record for futility is unmatched in baseball. For years, faithful Phillie fans had to read their morning paper upside down to get any satisfaction from the League Standings.

But in 1964, all that looked as if it were about to change. The Phils led the race much of the way, and when they took the field on September 21 against the Reds, they had a six-and-a-half-game margin with only 12 games left to play.

But they lost that day on what most observers would call a bonehead play: Chico Ruiz stole home while Frank Robinson, the Reds' best hitter, was up at bat. Had Ruiz failed, Robinson would have been deprived of a chance to drive in the winning run.

The Phils went on to lose the next day, and the next, and the next. By the time they finally won a game, they had dropped ten straight. The only solace for the Phillies was that by beating the Reds on the final day, they denied Cincinnati a tie for the flag.

As it turned out, the St. Louis Cardinals needed to win only one of their concluding three home games from the lowly Mets to clinch the pennant. Amazingly, they lost the first two and were behind in the third. At last, the Cards came to their senses, and realized whom they were playing against. St. Louis then went on to capture the flag Philadelphia figured to win.

A Star Is Born

As a youngster, he was thin and sickly. For the first four months of his life, he was given daily sun treatments to help subdue a severe case of rickets. One side of his chest was lower than the other; his bones had failed to develop properly.

"He was born sick," said Bob Gibson's mother, "and he got sicker. He had rickets, hay fever, asthma, pneumonia, and a rheumatic heart. I never thought he'd make it."

But in 1964, at the age of 28, Gibson, a 6-foot-1, 195-pounder, made it for real. The pennant race had been tight. The Cards came from behind to overhaul the Phillies and the Reds to win the National League pennant on the final day. In that exciting spurt it was Gibson's 19 victories that were telling.

If the pennant victory was hard fought, the World Series loomed as an even more difficult assignment. The Yankees, smarting from their shellacking at the hands of the Los Angeles Dodgers the previous year, were seeking to regain the world title. And their big guns were ready: Mickey Mantle, Roger Maris, Elston Howard, Joe Pepitone.

The Cards were exhausted from the pressure-packed climax of the pennant race. Among the weariest of the weary was Bob Gibson.

He had pitched twice in the final three days of the campaign. In his initial World Series assignment, the second game, Gibson was not at his best. The Yanks eased to an 8-3 triumph to draw even at one game apiece.

With the Series count again deadlocked 2-2, Cardinal manager Johnny Keane decided to go again with Gibson. This time, his righthanded ace responded with a 5-2 victory, which dragged out to 10 innings during which he struck out 13 batters.

In the sixth game, the Yanks bounced back to win 8-3. All

was in deadlock now; and No. 7, coming up, was life or death.

Keane called on Gibson again—this time with only two days' rest. Bob's opponent was Mel Stottlemyre, New York's outstanding rookie righthander.

For three innings, the pitchers hurled almost flawless ball. But in the fourth the Cards scored three runs; and in the fifth, they tallied three more to take a 6-0 lead.

But Gibson, taking deep breaths between almost every pitch, was starting to tire. In the sixth, the Yanks got to him for three runs, on singles by Bobby Richardson and Roger Maris and Mantle's home run into the left-field stands.

At this point, Keane conferred with Gibson, and then decided to leave him in. In the seventh frame, St. Louis boosted its margin to 7 to 3.

Then came the fateful ninth. Tom Tresh struck out. Clete Boyer homered. Pinch-hitter John Blanchard fanned for the second out, and then Phil Linz cut the Cards' lead to two runs, by hammering another four-bagger into the left-field seats.

Two pitchers were warming up in the Cards' bullpen. But Keane decided to stay with his starting pitcher for one more batter. Bobby Richardson approached the plate. Mantle and Maris were ominously standing by. But those redoubtable sluggers never got the chance, for Gibson, with the courage and talent that goes to make a champion, caused Richardson to lift an easy pop fly, gathered in effortlessly by second baseman Dal Maxvill.

In the final set-to, Gibson had fanned nine batters, lifting his total for the Series to 31—a postseason whiffing record which stood until Gibson himself topped it in 1968. He had brought St. Louis its first world's title in 18 years.

What Does a Guy Gotta Do?

On August 12, 1966, Art Shamsky stepped to the plate as a pinch-hitter for the Reds. It was the bottom of the eighth inning, and Cincinnati was locked in a 7-7 tie with Pittsburgh. Shamsky promptly unknotted the game by belting one out of Crosley Field.

But the Pirates came back with one run in the ninth to tie the game again and another in the tenth to go one ahead. Shamsky, who had been left in the game after his pinch-hit wallop, came up in the bottom of the tenth and hit another homer. It was now 9-9.

Pittsburgh scored two in the eleventh. But the Reds retaliated with two of their own—again on a Shamsky homer. Once again, the persistent Pirates came up with three runs in the thirteenth, and Shamsky did not get another chance for heroics.

Following this dazzling performance—three at bats, three homers, five RBI's—Shamsky returned to the bench. But on August 14, when he next came to bat as a pinch-hitter, he smacked still another home run, his fourth in four consecutive at-bats off four different pitchers. Though Art tied a major-league record, his prowess was still not enough to earn him a starting berth.

King of K's

The youngest man ever inducted into the Hall of Fame is Dodger lefthander Sandy Koufax. He came to Cooperstown at 36, an age at which most great players are still building their records. But an arthritic condition in his elbow forced Sandy to retire when he was only 31, at the acme of his career.

In his 12 years with the Dodgers, Koufax rose from an inept bonus baby to the best pitcher in baseball. Sandy came to Brooklyn straight off the campus of the University of Cincinnati, where he was known mostly for his talents in basketball.

In his first three years with the Dodgers he won only nine games. Everyone knew Sandy had a great fastball, but his inability to hold the bullet in the strike zone made baseball savants doubt whether he would ever become a star.

In 1959, Sandy showed the first sign that he might be something special when he struck out 18 men in one game, tying Bob Feller's record. That year, he won only eight games, and only eight the next, but he was surely on his way.

In 1961, he won 18 games and led the National League in strikeouts.

The following year, he won 14 games by mid-July, but he was put out of action until late September by a circulatory ailment. Still, he saw enough action to throw a no-hitter, to strike out 18 men for the second time, and to win the ERA crown.

Over the next four years, Sandy won 25, 19, 26, and 27, winning the ERA title each year and throwing three more no-hitters—his total now more than anyone else's in baseball history. The last no-hitter, hurled in 1965, was a perfect game against the Cubs. In that year he also established a new strikeout mark with 382 (since topped by Nolan Ryan).

In 1966, Sandy stunned the baseball world by retiring after a 27-9 season. The pain from the arthritis in his elbow was bearable, but not the prospect of disfigurement. Koufax's career was brief as big-league careers go, but it certainly was brilliant.

ON JUNE 9, 1966, the Minnesota Twins became the fourth team in major-league history to sock five homers *in one inning*! That's two more than the 1905 White Sox hit all season.

Cool, Calm, and Collected

You huddle in a corner of the dugout for seven or eight innings until the manager wags his finger toward you. Then you get the splinters out of your seat, walk over to the bat rack, and step up to home plate. The game is tight, or they wouldn't need you. You've only got three swings to do your stuff. No next time for you—get on base now, or else you're a bum.

It takes a pretty cool customer to be a pinch-hitter, and few men make a successful career of it. As a rule, the best men in a pinch have a few gray hairs on their heads—kids find it a little tougher to face the pressure day after day.

Smoky Burgess was 39 years old when he set the record for the most times reaching base as a pinch-hitter in one season—36 for the White Sox in 1966. Smoky started out as a catcher with the Cubs in 1949, but in his last few years, he rarely caught so much as an inning. In 1967, he appeared in 77 games and never once donned a mitt in earnest.

Dave Philley was 38 when he set the record for most consecutive pinch-hits. He got nine—eight in 1958, and one on his first time up the following year.

Three years later, at the age of 41, he established a new all-time mark by knocking out 24 pinch-hits in one season.

Pinch-hitting is one trick best learned by an old dog.

WHAT PRICE GLORY? About $30, if you ask Denny McLain. Before he hit the headlines with his 31 wins in 1968, McLain used to spend the off-season playing in the Puerto Rican Winter League. One night, after pitching his Mayaguez team to the championship, Denny was carried from the team bus on the shoulders of his adoring fans. While up there, however, his pocket was picked of $30.

Who Said Pitchers Can't Hit?

On July 3, 1966, Tony Cloninger was the nominee of the Atlanta Braves to pitch in Candlestick Park against the slugging San Francisco Giants. The young fireballer had won five of his previous six starts, and was fast making a name for himself as one of the most promising hurlers in the National League. But on this particular day, Cloninger was to make his name with a bat, a futile weapon in the hands of most hurlers.

Tony's teammates started pounding the ball in the top of the first inning and scored three runs. When Cloninger stepped to the plate with two outs, the bases were loaded with his Braves. Tony worked the count to three balls and two strikes, and then connected with a fastball and sent it sailing over the center-field fence, more than 410 feet away.

Armored with a seven-run lead before throwing a single pitch, Cloninger breezed through the San Francisco batting order for the first three innings. When he came to bat in the top of the fourth, Cloninger again found the bags full of Braves—this time again with two out. And again Cloninger walloped the ball for a homer!

Before the day was over, the Atlanta pitcher drove in another run with a single. He had driven in nine of his team's runs in a 17-3 victory and had become the first National Leaguer—and the first pitcher in either league—to hit two grand-slam home runs in a single game.

The No-Hitters That Weren't Good Enough

It's not easy to pitch a no-hit game and come out with nothing to show for it, but the feat has been accomplished surprisingly often.

The first man to go unrewarded for a mound masterpiece was Brooklyn's Sam Kimber, a 31-year-old rookie who on October 4, 1884, pitched 10 hitless innings against Toledo. But his mates failed to score; and when the game was called on account of darkness, Kimber had to content himself with a 0-0 tie. This experience so unnerved the poor man that he pitched only one game the following season, lost it, and quit baseball forever.

The first man to pitch a no-hitter and actually lose the game was Earl Moore of Cleveland. In 1901, he gave up no hits to Chicago through the first nine innings, but lost his touch in the tenth and bowed, 4-2.

Since 1901, this awful fate has befallen nine other pitchers, the most memorable victims being Hippo Vaughn and Harvey Haddix.

In 1917, the Cubs' Vaughn had the bad luck to face Fred Toney when the Red hurler was also pitching a no-hitter. In 1959, Haddix pitched 12 perfect innings for the Pirates only to lose in the 13th on the lone hit he allowed.

In addition to those nine unfortunates, consider the case of Steve Barber and Stu Miller, both of the Orioles. Pitching at home against the Tigers on April 30, 1967, Barber went 8⅔ innings without giving up a hit. He had, however, given up numerous free passes and one run. In the ninth, he yielded two walks and was visibly tiring. His wildness threatened to cost Baltimore the game. So manager Hank Bauer pulled his starter and brought in little Stu Miller, his ace reliever.

Miller came in with men on first and second, and promptly threw a wild pitch to advance the runners. The next batter hit a ground ball which was kicked by an infielder, as the lead run scored. Miller retired the next man to complete the no-hitter, but the Birds failed to score in their half of the ninth. Steve Barber sat in the dugout and watched in horror as his teammates pinned the loss on him.

Beantown Beauties

The American League has never had a more thrilling and chaotic pennant race than it did in 1967. Going into the final two days of the season, four teams still had a shot at winning, and the number of possible combinations that would result in a tie for the top spot was absolutely boggling.

Of the four clubs battling for the flag, the most unlikely was the Boston Red Sox, who only one year earlier had finished ninth. What separated the bums of '66 from the heroes of '67? The sudden blossoming of two players—pitcher Jim Lonborg and outfielder Carl Yastrzemski.

Lonborg, a 25-year-old righthander, went from a 10-10 record in 1966 to 22-9 in 1967. His excellent hurling won him the Cy Young award.

Yaz, on the other hand, did not blossom in quite the same way. He had given the Sox six solid years, winning the batting title in 1963. But in 1966, he had hit a mediocre .278, and for the sixth straight year he had failed to top 20 homers. Thus the baseball world was stunned when Yaz belted 44 homers and drove in 121 runs, as well as attaining his highest average ever— a thumping .326. All three marks were tops in the American League, earning the Boston outfielder the rarely achieved Triple Crown.

In the final two days of the campaign, the Sox squared off against the Twins. Yaz was simply unbelievable. He went 7-for-8 at the plate, including a game-winning homer, and in the final game, made a great throw to kill a Minnesota rally.

Lonborg was the winning pitcher that day, but he saved his best for the Series. On the mound against the Cardinals in the second game, he had a no-hitter going into the eighth; and he finished with a one-hit win, 5-0. The hitting, naturally, was supplied by Mr. Yastrzemski with two homers and four RBI's. Yaz hit yet another homer in the sixth game, and concluded the Series with a fat .400 average. Before losing the seventh game to Bob Gibson, Lonborg added a three-hit victory to his laurels.

It was quite a year for both of them, and quite a year for Bosox fans. Their team had come out of nowhere to give the city its first flag in 21 years.

AT 6'7" AND 285 LBS., Frank Howard is probably the biggest man who ever played in the big time. And in his years with the Washington Senators, he carried a mighty bat, too. Twice he led the league in homers, twice in total bases, and once in RBI's.

When big Frank was hot, there was no one hotter. During

May of 1968, in a span of six games, he poled out 10 round-trippers. No one has ever come close to this exploit.

Brock Rocks Sox

In the 1967 World Series, Cardinal Lou Brock was a one-man wrecking crew. In the opening game, he knocked out four hits to lead the Redbirds to a 2-1 win over Boston. Brock was a terror on the basepaths, stealing seven bases to break a record that had stood for 60 years. He stole three of the seven in the finale, as the Cards won 7-2. And among his 12 hits, he even belted an uncharacteristic home run.

Unbelievably, in the 1968 Series, Brock was an even better hitter. Once again he stole seven bases, but this time he collected 13 hits—two of them homers—to tie the all-time mark set by Bobby Richardson. This time, however, Lou's exploits were not enough to take the Cards past the victorious Tigers.

ON THE NIGHT of September 17, 1968, Gaylord Perry hurled a no-hitter against the St. Louis Cardinals at Candlestick Park. The Cardinals wasted no time exacting their revenge, as Ray Washburn set down the Giants without a hit on the following afternoon.

Never in the history of baseball had teams traded no-hitters on consecutive days. But like the four-minute mile, once the swap was accomplished, it suddenly became easy.

Next year, on April 30, Jim Maloney of Cincinnati held the Astros without a hit. On May 1—the very next day—Houston's Don Wilson returned the favor.

The Rise and Fall of Denny McLain

In 1968, Denny McLain had the kind of year a pitcher dreams about. He won 31 games for the Detroit Tigers, lost only six, and was a unanimous choice for both the Cy Young Award and Most Valuable Player honors. That year, the 24-year-old righthander became the first hurler to win 30 or more games since Dizzy Dean turned the trick back in 1934.

The following year, McLain was almost as good. He again led the league with 24 victories, and earned a share of the Cy Young Award with Baltimore's Mike Cuellar. McLain was a brash young man who was not well loved by his teammates, but he had so much ability that the Tigers wouldn't dream of trading him.

Then, in 1970, McLain's world began to come apart. He became implicated in a gambling operation, and was suspended from baseball by Commissioner Bowie Kuhn. When the suspension was lifted late in the year, McLain came back to find that his teammates scorned him, and on top of that misfortune, his stuff was gone. Perhaps due to his prolonged inactivity, McLain was able to manage only a 3-5 record.

So the Tigers shipped him to Washington, who needed a box-office attraction of McLain's ability. But now a more docile Denny provided neither—he won only 10 games and lost 22.

The Senators moved to Texas the next year, but they didn't take Denny with them. McLain moved on to Oakland, where he was shelled with such ferocity that he was demoted to the minors after pitching only five games. Later in the year, the Atlanta Braves took a gamble and picked up his contract. But the gamble was lost—McLain appeared in 15 games for the Braves, and posted an earned-run average of 6.50.

In 1973, McLain went to spring training with Atlanta, but he didn't make the team. Not yet 30, he went back to the minors to try to find his missing fastball. The 31-win season was only five years past, but it seemed an eternity ago.

WHETHER IT WAS because of transcontinental travel, a steady diet of night games, or because the hitters were all just lousy, in 1968 the American League was a pitcher's paradise. In that year, Boston's Carl Yastrzemski hit an uninspired .301 and led the league.

By contrast, in 1930, the entire roster of National League batsmen had a combined average of .303!

THROUGH MAY AND JUNE of 1968, Dodger pitcher Don Drysdale was untouchable. He hurled six straight shutouts, topping the mark of five set by Doc White in 1904. And his 58⅔ consecutive scoreless innings consigned Walter Johnson's record of 56 innings to second place.

But this incredible string of goose eggs was Don Drysdale's curtain call. Despite his early-season streak, he went on to post a mediocre record of 14-12. Next year, he was forced to retire in mid-season when his sore arm failed to come around.

Slipping the Cards a Mickey

The Year of the Pitcher: that's what everyone was calling 1968, and for good reason. The combined batting average for both leagues was .236, the lowest ever. Only 1,994 home runs were hit, as compared with nearly 3,000 six years earlier. And there were some superlative individual pitching performances: Don Drysdale's 58⅔ consecutive scoreless innings; Catfish Hunter's perfect game; Bob Gibson's 1.12 ERA; and Denny McLain's 31-6 record.

Appropriately, the 1968 World Series shaped up as the Series of the Pitcher. In the opener, St. Louis led with its ace, Bob Gibson, and Detroit started Denny McLain. But the great matchup did not live up to its promise. The Cards solved McLain for three early runs, and for all purposes the game was over. Meanwhile, the Tigers were so overpowered by Gibson that they not only failed to score, but they fanned 17 times to give Gibson a World Series record.

The Tigers came back to win the second game, 8-1, with Mickey Lolich on the hill; but the Cards won the next game rather easily, 7-3. Once again, the pitching matchup was Gibson vs. McLain. And once again, Gibson emerged on top, this time by a score of 10-1 as McLain was shelled from the mound in the third inning.

One game away from elimination, the Tigers called upon Lolich to keep their slim chances alive, and he did, 5-3.

Then McLain came back with two days' rest to win a laugher, 13-1.

In game seven, the unheralded Lolich continued his winning ways by topping Gibson 4-1. The portly lefthander had won three of his team's four victories, and he had stolen the limelight from his teammate McLain, whom everyone had expected to be the Tiger mainstay.

CURT BLEFARY was a busy young man on May 4, 1969. Playing for the Houston Astros, the first-sacker had a hand in seven double plays—a major-league record.

Amazin'!

On July 20, 1969, Neil Armstrong and Buzz Aldrin became the first men to set foot on the surface of the moon. But to baseball fans, the real miracle of 1969 occurred two months and four days later, when the New York Mets clinched the National League's Eastern Division crown.

For the first seven years of their existence, the Mets had been the doormat of the league, never finishing higher than ninth and averaging over 100 defeats a year. But by mid-June of 1969, largely on the strength of an 11-game winning streak, the Mets attained the .500 mark for the first time in their history. Though this in itself was cause for celebration, the Mets continued to win through July and August, and seemed sure of finishing in the first division.

In mid-August, New York was in second place, nine and a half games behind the Chicago Cubs, who seemed sure to win their first title in 24 years. But the Mets closed with an amazing rush; they won 35 of their last 45 games, while the Cubs collapsed.

The Mets won the title on superb pitching, tight defense, and timely hitting by many players who had never hit so well before.

In the N.L. playoffs against the Atlanta Braves, the Mets changed their formula for victory. Their pitching faltered, but their bats exploded for 27 runs in three games, and the Mets swept into the World Series.

Before the season, Las Vegas gamblers had quoted odds of 100-1 against the Mets making it this far. And even in October, they were still heavy underdogs to the powerful Orioles, who had run away with the American League race.

When the Mets lost the first game with their ace, 25-game-winner Tom Seaver, on the mound, the picture looked bleak, indeed. Many Met fans figured that their club had at last run out of miracles. But Jerry Koosman won the second game 2-1, holding the Birds hitless until the seventh.

Then it was on to New York, and a three-game sweep to the championship. Donn Clendenon belted three round-trippers in the five games to tie a record; Al Weis hit .455 (including the tying homer in the fifth game); Jerry Koosman won two of the four Met victories; and each member of the Met outfield—Tommie Agee, Cleon Jones, Ron Swoboda—made at least one fielding play that would have been the gem of any World Series.

The Mets had capped baseball's first 100 years with perhaps the most improbable and exciting performance ever.

Neatness Pays

The Milwaukee Braves had lost two of the first three games of the 1957 World Series, and were in imminent danger of losing the fourth despite the fact that their ace, Warren Spahn, was on the mound. The Yankees had pushed a run across the plate in the top

of the tenth, and the Braves were just three outs away from ex-
tinction.

The first batter due up in the Braves' tenth was Spahn, a
good hitter for a pitcher, but still only a pitcher—not a slugger.
Manager Fred Haney sent up Nippy Jones, a journeyman first-
baseman, as a pinch-hitter. Jones had toiled in the minors until
the Braves' regular first-baseman broke a leg midway through the
campaign.

On the mound for the Yankees was Tommy Byrne, an aging
but still effective lefty. His first pitch to Jones was in the dirt, and
got by catcher Yogi Berra. Jones started toward first base, claim-
ing that the pitch had hit him. The umpire said it was merely
ball one, and called him back. Jones argued to no avail, then
walked toward the backstop and retrieved the ball. He thrust the
ball in the umpire's face and told him to look at the shoe-polish
stain. Confronted with this unassailable evidence, the ump
awarded Jones first base.

The fans were roaring with pleasure at the ump's decision
to reverse himself. Things were looking up for the Braves, and
the Yanks were rattled.

A new pitcher was now sent in, but Johnny Logan greeted

him with a double, and Eddie Mathews followed with a homer to win the contest. The Braves had pulled game four out of the fire, and went on to win the Series in seven games.

Veteran baseball observers could not recall having seen the shoe-polish play before, and no one was to see it again until 1969.

The scene was the fifth game of the World Series between the New York Mets and the Baltimore Orioles. The Mets were down 3-0 in this game. If they lost it, they would have to travel to Baltimore to conclude the Series.

In the sixth inning, the Mets' leadoff man is a fella named —you guessed it—Jones. The pitch comes in low, Cleon Jones claims first base, the ump says no, but here comes the ball, marked with the telltale shinola. Jones goes to first base, scores on a homer, and the Mets go on to win the game and the Series.

For shoe-polish dramatics, there's no keeping up with the Joneses.

Et Tu, Baseball?

You could hardly be blamed if the name of Cesar Gutierrez does not ring a bell. In four big-league seasons, the Venezuelan infielder played in as many as 100 games in only one season, and he never hit over .245.

But for one glorious day, Cesar conquered baseball. In the second game of a doubleheader on June 21, 1970, he came to bat for the Tigers seven times and banged out seven hits.

Lady Luck did not continue to hail Cesar. The very next year, he found himself back in the minors.

IN 1970, PITTSBURGH fans must have wondered whether the front office had stocked the bullpen by going to the butcher shop. Three of the Pirate pitchers that year were named Moose, Lamb, and Veale.

ON APRIL 22, 1970, Tom Seaver of the Mets was on the mound in the sixth inning of a game against the San Diego Padres. Two men were out, and up to this point, Seaver had fanned nine while allowing no runs—a super game, certainly, but no cause for re-writing the record books.

But when Seaver got his last out in the ninth, he made pitching history. Tom had fanned the last 10 men he faced, a new major-league mark. And those 10, coupled with the nine he had fanned through the first 6⅔ innings, gave him a total of 19 for the game, tying the record set by Steve Carlton one year earlier.

Comedy of Errors

The 1970 World Series supplied the match all baseball fans had been waiting for—the powerhouse of the American League, the Baltimore Orioles, against the Big Red Machine of Cincinnati. Each team had won its divisional title handily, and each had swept to the pennant by taking three straight games in its divisional playoff.

Pitchers Jim Palmer of the Birds and Gary Nolan of the Reds battled on even terms through the first five innings, each allowing three runs. After Baltimore went down quietly in the top of the sixth, Cincinnati seemed ready to erupt in its half of that inning.

The first batter up, Lee May, ripped a line drive down the third-base line, a sure double. But Brooks Robinson threw himself in the path of the ball and nabbed it for out one. The Reds didn't know it yet, but this was the kind of play Brooks was to make seem routine as the Series progressed.

But to get back to the bottom of the sixth—the next batter up, Bernie Carbo, drew a base on balls from the rattled Palmer. Carbo hustled to third as the next man singled, and Palmer was only one hit away from a shower.

Pinch-hitter Ty Cline then hit a Palmer fastball straight down against the infield to the left of home plate. The ball shot up off the artificial surface, and seemed to take an eternity before commencing its downward flight.

As catcher Ellie Hendricks waited for the ball to come down, Carbo foolishly raced toward the plate with what would be the tie-breaking run. Umpire Ken Burkhart, not figuring on Carbo to come home, planted himself along the line to make a call of fair or foul as Hendricks caught the ball.

What a tableau! Carbo sliding into home, Hendricks lunging to make the tag, and Burkhart caught between them. In the three-way collision that ensued, umpire Burkhart was sent flying into the air. He landed with his right thumb extended, thus precipitating a rhubarb. As always, the victimized party argued to no avail.

In the next inning, Brooks Robinson hit a homer to ice the game for the Orioles, 4-3.

The next day, photos in the paper revealed what had actually occurred in the bizarre play. Carbo slid home, *but he never touched the plate.* Hendricks made the tag with the glove, *but he had the ball in his other hand.* Burkhart made the call, *but his spill turned him around so that he was facing the outfield and could not possibly have seen the play.*

Understandably demoralized by this comedy of errors, the Big Red Machine sputtered to a five-game Series defeat.

On June 23, 1971, Rick Wise took the mound against the powerful Reds in their own ballpark. Pitching for the last-place Phils, Rick didn't count on his teammates for much batting support. So he held the Reds hitless, and clouted two home runs himself!

Ouch!

Whether Montreal second baseman Ron Hunt was fearless or brainless did not really concern manager Gene Mauch. For Hunt's black-and-blue body became an integral part of the Expo offense in 1971. The scrappy second-baseman reached first 50 times as a result of being hit by a pitch. That's a record few will try to top.

Return from Oblivion

For ups and downs, not even the roller coaster at Coney Island can top the tale of Luis Tiant. For four years, the Cuban right-hander pitched for the Cleveland Indians in relative obscurity. Then, in 1968, he burst upon the baseball scene by winning 21 games while losing only nine. In that year, he was the American League starter in the All-Star game, and finished the season with an earned-run average of 1.60, the lowest since Walter Johnson's 1.49 in 1919.

Tiant seemed to have a brilliant future ahead of him. But the very next year, he came up with a sore arm. Instead of repeating his performance of 1968, he virtually reversed his record, winning nine while losing 20.

Between seasons, Luis was traded to Minnesota. When the Twins saw that Tiant couldn't throw hard enough to break a pane of glass, they shipped him to Boston. There he compiled a dismal record of 1-7, whereupon the Sox gave him, at the end of 1971, an outright release.

The following year, Tiant hooked on with Richmond in the Atlanta farm system. But his performance was so undistinguished that even the pitching-poor Braves refused to pick up his contract.

Back in the A.L., however, Boston was equally deficient in able moundsmen, and had a slim chance to cop a flag. The Sox decided to give Tiant a try. Miraculously, Luis rediscovered his fastball in Fenway Park, and took the Red Sox to within half a game of the Eastern Division crown.

Tiant was 15-6 for the year, but won 11 of 12 after July, when the chase for the flag was really hot. Six of these wins were shutouts. With a mark of 1.91, Tiant emerged once more as the ERA king.

ON SEPTEMBER 19, 1972, almost everybody got into the act during a game between the Oakland A's and the Chicago White Sox. In that extravaganza, a procession of 51 players circulated between the dugout, the diamond, and the showers.

That day, the egalitarian A's sent 30 men into the fray. The more moderate Sox restrained themselves to a mere 21 entrants. Though the game went 15 innings, nobody had been on the field long enough to get tired. The official scorekeeper, however, was pooped to a palsy.

One-Man Gang

Steve Carlton of the St. Louis Cardinals was an intractable hold-out, and so was Rick Wise of the Philadelphia Phillies. Each pitcher had completed a highly successful 1971 season, and each wanted a lot more money than the club felt he was worth. What to do? The Cardinal general manager sat down with the Phillie general manager, and they arrived at a solution: trade one problem for the other.

And what a solution that proved to be for the Phils! While Wise was having an average season over at St. Louis, Carlton became the most phenomenal Phillie since Grover Cleveland Alexander. He led the National League in wins, ERA, strikeouts, games started, and games completed, and he won the Cy Young award. During one stretch of 63 innings, Carlton allowed only one earned run.

But the most amazing aspect of Carlton's great year is the fact that while he won 27 games, the rest of the Phillie staff won only 32. In other words, during 1972, Steve Carlton won 45% of all the games won by the last-place Phils.

Old Sarge

When pitcher Hoyt Wilhelm broke in with the 1952 Giants, he broke in with style. The 29-year-old rookie reliever won 15 games while losing only 3, and his knuckler won him the ERA crown. For good measure, he hit a homer his first time up.

Wilhelm's butterfly continued to baffle N.L. hitters until 1957, when he was traded to Cleveland in the American League. In 1958, it seemed the Old Sarge was through—he had just posted a mark of 3-10, but more important, he was now 35 years old.

Yet Wilhelm went on to show that he had more lives than a cat. He hooked on with the Orioles as a starting pitcher, and in 1959 he won 15 games. He also took the earned-run-average title with a 2.19—the only man to lead each league in ERA. For good measure this time, he tossed a no-hitter against the Yankees.

The next year, Wilhelm returned to the bullpen, where he starred for Baltimore until 1963. But the Orioles didn't want to keep a 39-year-old geezer on their staff—his arm might fall off any moment. So they sent him on to Chicago, where he had six of his very best years.

After a brief sojourn with the Angels (California, not Heavenly), the old man returned to the National League, after an absence of 13 years. In 1970, at the age of 47, he relieved in 50 games for the Atlanta Braves, winning six and losing four.

By the time Hoyt hung up his spikes in 1972, he had pitched in 1,070 games over a span of 21 years. No one, not even Cy Young, appeared in so many games. When the book was closed on Old Sarge, it was quite a relief to big-league batters.

Pride of Pittsburgh

On September 30, 1972, Roberto Clemente smacked a double to left-center off the Mets' Jon Matlack. A roar went up from the Pittsburgh crowd as the message was flashed on the scoreboard that the Puerto Rican star had just banged out the 3,000th hit of his illustrious career.

No one could have known that this would be his last hit in regular-season play. In December of that year, Clemente boarded a plane for Nicaragua. He never made it. Overloaded with supplies for the victims of the Managua earthquake, the plane crashed into the waters off San Juan. Puerto Rico lost its most famous citizen, and baseball lost one of its real greats.

During his 18 years in a Pirate uniform, Clemente led the National League in batting four times, twice with an average of better than .350. Over a full career, he hit .317.

In 1966, he was voted the league's Most Valuable Player; but year in, year out, he always ranked high in the balloting. Roberto was so extraordinary a right-fielder that he won a Golden Glove for 12 consecutive years, a feat matched only by Willie Mays.

Clemente reached the apex of his career with his performance in the 1971 World Series against the Orioles. In the Bucs' seven-game victory, Roberto batted a rousing .414, slammed out two homers, and made spectacular catches and throws which defy description.

A few months after Clemente's death, he was inducted into the Hall of Fame.

Silencing the Critics

Johnny Bench of the Cincinnati Reds is undoubtedly the brightest young star in baseball today. At the age of 20, he was the Reds' regular backstop, and he commanded the respect of even veteran pitchers with his savvy and agility behind the plate.

In 1970, when 22, Big John won Most Valuable Player honors as he led the Reds to the flag. He led the league with 45 homers and 148 runs batted in. Writers said he could one day rank with Dickey, Cochrane, Campanella, and Berra; some said that he was already better than any of those four Hall-of-Famers.

In 1971, Bench hit only .258, and the Reds did not repeat as National League champs. Accolades from the press were heavily outweighed by complaints that early stardom had gone to Johnny's head, that he now considered himself to be a personality rather than a ballplayer.

Next season, however, Bench showed his critics what kind of a ballplayer he was. He again led the league in homers and RBI's, again won the MVP, and again led the Reds to the Series. And he was still not even 25 years old!

In 1972, the Expos' Mike Marshall earned a place in the first rank of National League firemen by winning 14 games, saving 18, and posting a neat ERA of 1.78. And in 1973, he was even better, winning 14 and saving 31 while appearing in 92 games—a new major-league record.

You can bet that as Marshall was putting out all those fires, there were some flaming red faces in the front offices of Detroit, Seattle, and Houston. Mike had pitched for each of these three clubs (Seattle later moved to Milwaukee), and each club had given up on him and let him go.

Yet Montreal, too, let Marshall go, despite his great 1973 season. And Mike embarrassed the Expo brass by starring for L.A. in 106 games, a new record, and leading his mates to the Series.

Instant Hero

As the 1972 World Series opened in Cincinnati, Oakland catcher Fury Gene Tenacci—known as Gene Tenace to those few who had heard of him at all—was an unlikely prospect for stardom. He had spent the first half of the regular season collecting splinters on the A's bench, and cracked the lineup only when Dave Duncan, the number one catcher, suddenly forgot how to hit in the closing two months. Given this opportunity, Tenace didn't exactly distinguish himself at the plate, either—he hit .225, collecting only five homers.

In the American League playoff against Detroit, Tenace was a complete bust, both at the plate and behind it, until he hit a single to drive in a run in the final game. Up to that point, he had gone 0-for-15.

Tenace's single must have injected new life into his tired bat, for in the first game of the World Series, he knocked two serves by Reds' pitcher Gary Nolan over the fence. Tenace's two clouts provided all the A's runs in a 3-2 victory.

In the fourth game, Gene hit another homer, and the A's went on to pull out another 3-2 thriller. He also contributed a key single to the ninth-inning rally in which the A's scored the deciding two runs.

In game five, the Reds jumped out to an early 1-0 lead. But when Gene Tenace came to bat in the second inning, he found two of his mates on board, and he promptly blasted the ball over the fence. This was his fourth Series homer, tying a record held by Babe Ruth, Lou Gehrig, Duke Snider, and Hank Bauer. However, the A's could not hold the lead. The Series went to game 6, which the Reds won 8-1.

Showdown: game seven, winner take all. In the first inning, Tenace came to bat with a man on third and two down. Predictably by now, he delivered the run with a single. But the Reds knotted the game in the fifth, forcing Tenace to go to work again. He doubled a man home for his ninth RBI of the Series, and Oakland was given a lead it did not relinquish. The A's won 3-2, and were champions of the world.

Fury Gene Tenacci had come out of nowhere to dominate a Series as few ever have. He hadn't figured in the A's plans at the start of the season, but he sure did at the end.

As EXPECTED, the designated-hitter rule which the American League adopted for the 1973 campaign resulted in more hitting. But the principal beneficiary of the new rule was the starting pitcher, who no longer had to be removed for a pinch-hitter in the late innings of a game in which he was tied or behind.

As a result, in 1973, 12 American League pitchers won 20 or more games, as compared with only one pitcher in the National League, which declined to institute the designated-hitter rule.

Out of the Hospital and into the Series

As the New York Mets closed spring training in 1973, they figured that they had a pretty good shot at the Eastern Division crown. Though on paper the Pirates still looked stronger, they would be without the late Roberto Clemente for the first time since 1955, and no one could yet estimate the severity of that loss.

The Mets broke well from the gate; but as May rolled around, their injury jinx of the previous two years was returning in spades. First-baseman John Milner pulled a hamstring and had to watch the proceedings from the sidelines for more than two weeks in the midst of a batting streak. Pitcher Jon Matlack was struck in the forehead by a line drive, and suffered a fracture of the skull. Catcher Jerry Grote's arm was broken by a pitch, and he was out for more than two months. Left-fielder Cleon Jones broke a bone in his hand, and missed two months. Short-stop Bud Harrelson broke a bone, too, and was sidelined for four weeks.

As the season wore on, the injuries kept on coming. Reserve outfielder George Theodore suffered a dislocated hip in a collision with center-fielder Don Hahn. Harrelson broke another bone, this time the sternum. And throughout it all, right-fielder Rusty Staub played almost every day with two banged-up hands that pained him every time he took a full cut at the ball. For the whole season, the Mets' power hitter was reduced to a singles hitter.

No team could have borne up under such a run of injuries, and the Amazin' Mets didn't either. They were more than 10 games back long after the All-Star break. On August 30, they were in last place. In the last week of the season, they were still under .500.

Yet when the season ended on October 2, there were the Mets, sitting in first place. How did it happen? A lot of cooperation from four other clubs, all of whom were still in contention until the last days of the race, plus a little of that old Met magic.

The Amazin' Mets went into the divisional playoffs with no 20-game winner, no .300 hitter, and no man who had driven in as many as 80 runs. Yet again, they defied both logic and the oddsmakers as they took the measure of Cincinnati's Big Red Machine in five games. As in the race for the divisional title, they once again demonstrated that it is not always the best team on paper that wins the ballgame.

Unlike 1969, however, the Met magic was not strong enough to carry them through the World Series. New York won three of the first five games, and was in position to deliver the knockout blow to the Oakland A's, but the K.O. punch never came. The defending champions won the last two games in their own ball-park, and the year of the underdog was over.

HENRY AARON's season-long chase of Babe Ruth's career record of 714 home runs left obscured a truly remarkable 1973 season. At the age of 39, Hammerin' Hank hit .301, knocked in 96 runs, and belted 40 homers—more than anyone his age had ever hit. When *he* was 39, the Babe hit only 22 round-trippers.

Ya Gotta Have Heart

Lefty John Hiller was in his sixth season as a middle-inning re-liever and spot starter for the Tigers. Between 1965 and 1970, he had labored with only sporadic success, winning 23 games while losing 19.

Suddenly, the career of the 27-year-old hurler seemed to be over, hardly before it had had a chance to blossom. Hiller was struck down by a heart attack.

After sitting out the entire 1971 season, in 1972 John per-suaded his doctors to let him pitch batting practice. His siege had left him 40 pounds lighter, but no weaker. He discovered that, if anything, the velocity of his fastball had improved, and so had his control. Hiller proved so effective in batting practice that man-ager Billy Martin agreed to restore him to the active roster. Pitching in 24 games, John won only one and saved three, but he compiled an ERA of 2.05, his best ever.

In 1973, Martin made Hiller his number one lefthanded reliever. And Hiller responded by becoming the number one re-liever in the whole league. He won 10 games, and saved 38—an all-time record.

NEED A GUIDE around baseball's cellar?

Then Philadelphia's the place to go. Totaled together, the two teams of the City of Brotherly Love had wound up in last place 42 times by 1973. Each club holds the all-time record for finishing last in its league.

In the National League, the Phillies have leased the basement 24 times, while the Athletics hit the bottom in 17 seasons, until they left for Kansas City in 1955. Out there, the A's finished last five more times before moving to Oakland in 1968.

In 1955, Detroit's Al Kaline was the top batter in the American League, posting a mark of .340. He was only 20 years old, the youngest player ever to win the title in either league. Though Kaline played for 19 more years and frequently hit over .300, he never again won the batting crown. He did, however, amass 3,007 hits, a total surpassed by only 11 other players.

They Used to Kick Sand in His Face

Dave Johnson had been the Orioles' regular second-baseman for seven years, mostly on the strength of his excellent fielding. But in 1972, he had his worst year at the plate, batting a dismal .221.

At 30 years of age, the front-office figured, he could not be counted on to bounce back to his .282 mark of the previous year. So during the winter, Baltimore traded Johnson to the Atlanta Braves in exchange for Earl Williams, who was expected to supply some much-needed power.

But overnight, so it seemed, it was Johnson who blossomed into a power hitter, poling out 43 round-trippers. This was 38

225

more homers than he had hit in 1972, and 25 more than he had ever hit before. In fact, Johnson broke the record for most homers hit by a second-baseman, set in 1922 by Rogers Hornsby.

Charlie O. Gets His Comeuppance

The 1973 World Series was exciting, but the events on the field were overshadowed by the weird events off the field.

Before the Series opened, the owner of the A's, Charles O. Finley, requested permission from the Mets to fill the vacant 25th spot on his roster with second-baseman Manny Trillo, who had joined the club too late to be eligible for postseason play. Finley got himself into this fix by peddling catcher José Morales to Montreal in mid-September.

The Mets felt that Finley should lie in the bed he had made for himself, and refused to declare Trillo eligible. Charlie O. was so enraged that, on the day of the Series opener, he had the public-address announcer tell the fans what poor sports the Mets were.

The second game was won by the Mets with the aid of two errors made in the 11th inning by reserve second-baseman Mike Andrews. Now, Finley was really boiling, for Andrews' primary role had been as a righthanded pinch-hitter: his fielding had always been suspect. If Trillo had been on the roster, *he* would have been playing second—not Andrews.

A half-hour after the game, Finley finagled Andrews into taking a "physical" from the team doctor. The medic promptly declared that Andrews' shoulder made him unfit to play. Immediately upon hearing this, Finley requested Andrews to sign the doctor's report, so that Mike could be put on the disabled list. Then Finley would be enabled once more to approach the Mets and ask for that club's permission to let Trillo play.

But according to Andrews, his shoulder was just fine, and he told Finley and Finley's doctor that he would not sign the prepared statement. Finley told Mike that if he really wanted to "help the team," he would go along with the maneuver and open a spot for Trillo. Humiliated by the whole procedure, Andrews signed the paper and went home to Massachusetts.

The Mets turned the matter over to Commissioner Bowie Kuhn, who investigated the circumstances and made all the facts known. Andrews was reinstated.

Oakland manager Dick Williams had had many run-ins with Finley himself. Just before the third game, Williams announced that after the Series he would quit the A's.

The next day, Andrews rejoined his teammates in New York. That night, Andrews made a dramatic appearance as a pinch-hitter. As he came to the plate, 55,000 Met fans gave the 30-year-old infielder a standing ovation. And more cheers followed as he returned to the dugout. The only man in the stadium not on his feet was Charles O. Finley.

Put That in Your Pipe

The merits of synthetic surfaces, such as Astro Turf and Tartan Turf, have been the topic of heated discussion ever since they were introduced in Houston's Astrodome. When asked what he thought of artificial grass, New York Mets' reliever Tug McGraw neatly elevated himself above the controversy. "I don't really know," Tug said. "I never smoked the stuff."

The Home Run King

Henry Aaron entered the 1974 baseball season with 713 home runs, only one short of the prodigious total compiled by Babe Ruth. That Henry would surpass the Babe was no longer in doubt; all that remained to be seen was when he would do it. Many a hitter has been stricken by a severe slump as he neared a record.

But Henry Aaron wasted no time. At Cincinnati's Riverfront Stadium, on his very first swing on opening day, he smashed a drive into the left-field stands. Jack Billingham had the distinction of delivering that gracious serve.

Aaron went hitless the next day; but on Monday night, April 8, he rewarded his fans in Atlanta with a four-base blast off Al Downing of the Dodgers. For the figure filberts, home run number

715 came in the fourth inning, at 9:07, with one man on base. It was Henry's first official at bat in Atlanta.

Aaron's sense of drama did not end there. In his very last trip to the plate in 1974—and his last appearance as a Brave—he hit a home run. It was his 20th of the season, and the 733rd of his long and glorious career.

Stop, Thief!

When Maury Wills established a new stolen-base record by copping 104 in 1962, many baseball experts felt that this mark would stand for years, and certainly would not be challenged by any of the current crop of ballplayers.

Twelve years later, a man who had been an outfielder for the Chicago Cubs in 1962 shattered Wills' record by pilfering 118 bags. This remarkable man was Lou Brock, a St. Louis Cardinal.

The Longest Single

It's pretty hard to think of a 25-year-old as a candidate for Comeback Player of the Year. Yet in 1974, Philadelphia's Mike Schmidt came back from a disastrous rookie season to become the National League's home-run champ—and incidentally, the unofficial holder of the record for the game's longest single.

In 1973, Mike got off to a slow start and just kept getting slower as the season wore on. His season-long slump produced an anemic .196 batting average, compounded by 136 strikeouts.

However, in 1974, Schmidt broke from the gate fast, as did the Phillie team. For almost the whole year, he kept his batting average over .300, though he finally slipped to .282, and he finished with a league-leading 36 homers. His RBI total of 116 was second only to Johnny Bench, and his 108 runs left him two short of Pete Rose's highwater mark.

As for the longest single—it came in Houston's Astrodome on June 10. As soon as Schmidt made contact with the pitch, everyone in the park knew it was destined to be a tape-measure homer. After the game, Houston centerfielder Cesar Cedeno said, "I knew the ball was going out. I gave up on it, but I kept running back because I wanted to see how far it would go. I never saw a ball hit so high and so far."

Then, a crash, and the ball dropped at Cedeno's feet. It had hit a public-address speaker 329 feet from home plate, 117 feet above the field. No ground rule had ever been formulated regarding such a matter. No one ever conceived the notion that a batted ball might ever strike the contraption.

In any event, Schmidt's ball did. What geometricians later declared would have been a 500-foot homer dropped in center field. Cedeno picked it up, fired the ball to second base, and prevented Schmidt from advancing beyond first.

Though Schmidt was deprived of his homer, his teammates did not miss the run too much, for they were on their way to a 12-0 victory.

IN ST. LOUIS, before a game with the Cards, Met manager Yogi Berra was interviewed on the air by veteran announcer Jack Buck. At the conclusion of the program, Buck handed Yogi a check made out "Payable to Bearer."

Yogi thanked Jack, glanced at the check, and then looked up forlornly. "Jack," he said disappointedly, "you know me all these years, and you still don't know how to spell my name."

The New Dynasty

By winning the 1974 World Series, the Oakland A's became the only team besides the Yankees to take three titles in a row. On paper, the A's are not nearly as impressive as the Yanks of old; indeed, on paper they were less impressive than the Reds, whom they beat in 1972, and the Dodgers, whom they whipped in 1974. But ballgames are not won on paper. On the field, the A's just went out and won.

There is perhaps no better illustration of how the A's managed than in their first game of the Series with the Dodgers. The A's were outhit 11 to 6; their starting pitcher, Ken Holtzman, did not survive the fifth inning, while L.A.'s Andy Messersmith hurled eight solid frames; the A's even made two errors to the Dodgers' one. Nevertheless, the A's won the game 3-2.

The A's went on to win the Series in five games. Each game was close—four of the five ended in a score of 3-2—but in the pinch, the young Dodgers broke down time and again. The A's never did.

Who Says Thirteen's Unlucky?

When California's Ed Figueroa stopped Kansas City 6-2, the victory marked the Angels' first win over the Royals in their last thirteen meetings in 1975. And what's more, Figueroa finally figured out how to retire third-baseman George Brett, who had reached him for thirteen straight hits.

The date of this event? September 13.

WHEN PITTSBURGH clobbered the Cubs 22-0 near the end of the 1975 season, it marked the most lopsided shutout defeat since 1883, when Providence overwhelmed Philadelphia 28-0. What made the defeat even harder to take for the Cubs was that it took place in the supposedly friendly confines of Wrigley field.

Those diehard Cub fans who stuck it out to the end were rewarded by witnessing one of the greatest days at bat any player had ever had. Pirate second-baseman Rennie Stennett stepped to the plate seven times and produced seven hits—four singles, a double, and a triple. Only one other man in the history of the game had ever gone 7-for-7 in a nine-inning game: Wilbert Robinson of the old Baltimore Orioles in 1892.

You'd think Stennett's bat would have been a bit tired after all that heavy thumping, but no—the next day, Rennie came back to get three more hits, establishing a modern-day record of 10 hits in two games.

230

Cloudy Crystal Ball

San Francisco pitcher John "Count" Montefusco enjoyed a most productive freshman season: 15 wins, a 2.88 ERA, and 215 strike-outs, second in the league to Tom Seaver. Montefusco's exploits resulted in his being selected 1975 National League Rookie-of-the-Year.

But the cocky "Count of Monte Frisco," as he has been dubbed by his fans, took some lumps on the way to his laurels. After beating the Cubs in mid-July to lift his record to 10-4, the Count said he "couldn't wait till we play the Reds next week. . . . I'm going to shut them out. . . . I'm going to strike out Johnny Bench four times." Shades of Dizzy Dean!

On July 31, Cincinnati's Riverfront Stadium was packed with Red rooters who wanted to see the Count make good or eat his words. The latter proved the case, as the Reds tallied in the first inning and exploded for six runs in the second. The Count was driven into exile in the showers.

The Red rally was highlighted by a 460-foot, three-run homer off the bat of . . . Johnny Bench.

Attendance Woes

In 1975, fans at San Francisco's Candlestick Park were so few and far between that Giant right-fielder Bobby Murcer commented, "If they check the upper deck, they might find Patty Hearst hiding out."

ON THE FINAL DAY of the 1975 season, the California Angels gave dramatic evidence of their year-long batting anemia. Facing four Oakland pitchers, the Angels' batsmen failed to get a hit against any of them.

The four A's hurlers—Vida Blue, Glen Abbott, Paul Lindblad, Rollie Fingers—shared pitching duties in an attempt to give all a final tuneup before the American League championship playoffs with the Red Sox. The result of their tuneup was one of the strangest no-hitters ever: the first to be thrown by four men, and only the third to involve more than one pitcher. (The other two are the Babe Ruth-Ernie Shore "perfect" game of 1917 and the Steve Barber-Stu Miller duet of 1967, which ended in a loss.)

Auspicious Debut

It's hard to imagine anyone having a finer rookie year than Fred Lynn had in 1975. The Boston Red Sox center-fielder played marvelous defense, ran the bases like a veteran, and was up among the league leaders in virtually every batting category. He led the league in runs scored (103), in doubles (47), and in slugging percentage (.566); he finished second in batting average (.331), and third in RBI's (105); he connected for 21 home runs; and most important, he sparked his team to a division title, league pennant, and very nearly a World Series crown.

No freshman in memory had ever done *so many* things so well. That's probably why Lynn won American League Rookie-of-the-Year honors so convincingly over his teammate Jim Rice, who had similarly impressive batting statistics.

It was on June 18, 1975 that Lynn made the transition from promising rookie to nascent star. Two nights earlier, he had seen his 20-game hitting skein snapped. This game with Detroit was to make up for whatever disappointment he might have felt. Lynn came to the plate six times and collected five hits—a single, a triple, and three homers. His triple missed clearing the wall by only three feet. Lynn's 16 total bases were good for 10 RBI's as Boston walloped the Tigers 15-1.

During the hot-stove season, the baseball writers made official what everyone who had followed American League baseball already knew—that Fred Lynn was not only the top rookie of the year, but also the top player. Lynn became the first rookie ever to win the Most Valuable Player award.

A sidelight on this great achievement: while Red Sox scouts and most other baseball pundits fully expected Lynn to become a major-league regular, none expected such a spectacular debut. In 1974 at Pawtucket, Boston's top farm club, Lynn had hit only .282; and in the previous year at Bristol, his batting average was a mere .259!

ON JULY 21, 1975, Felix Millan of the New York Mets stroked four singles—in the first inning, the third, the sixth, and the eighth. Try as he might, on none of these occasions was he able to reach second. Each time, lumbering Joe Torre erased him by grounding into a double play!

Joe's dubious feat has no parallel in National League annals, but he does have to share "honors" with two American Leaguers: both Goose Goslin of the Senators, in 1934, and Mike Kreevich of the White Sox, in 1939, also hit into four DP's in one game.

HOUSTON RELIEF PITCHER José Sosa had a lot to crow about after the Astros whipped the Pittsburgh Pirates, 8-4. Sosa, called up from the International League in July, not only picked up his first major-league save, but he also hit a three-run homer in his first big-league at-bat!

What made this feat even more remarkable was the fact that—because of the designated-hitter rule employed by the International League—Sosa had not previously had a bat in his hands all year!

Top Credentials

At the conclusion of a disappointing 1975, Atlanta Braves' General Manager Eddie Robinson stated that he was seeking a "fiery, enthusiastic" type for his next field manager. Later that month, he called a press conference to announce the hiring of Dave

Bristol, former manager of the Cincinnati Reds and the Milwaukee Brewers.

One reporter, recalling Robinson's earlier pronouncement, asked Bristol if he were a fiery type.

"I guess so," replied Bristol. "I've been fired three times."

EACH YEAR, 24 baseball writers — two from each league city — are given responsibility for selecting the league's Cy Young Award winner. Rarely have the writers been confronted with as difficult a choice as the National League scribes had in 1975. Although their pick was Tom Seaver (for the third time), a compelling case could have been made for any of four candidates.

Seaver, bouncing back from a disappointing 11-11 season

marred by injury, posted a won-lost record of 21-9. He led the league in strikeouts with 243, and notched an ERA of 2.38, third in the league. The Met ace was also third among National League moundsmen in shutouts, complete games, and innings pitched. And striking out more than 200 batters for the eighth straight year, he broke a record he had shared with Walter Johnson and Rube Waddell.

Randy Jones, who finished second in the balloting, enjoyed a comeback even more spectacular than Seaver's. The young San Diego hurler's 1974 log showed 8 wins, 22 losses, and a stratospheric ERA of 4.46. Contrast those figures with his 1975 stats: 20 wins, only 12 losses, a league-leading ERA of 2.24, six shutouts, and two one-hitters! Jones was also second in complete games and innings pitched.

Al Hrabosky of the St. Louis Cardinals emerged as the top fireman in the league, posting 22 saves, 13 wins, and a sparkling ERA of 1.67 in 65 games. He carried the shaky Card pitching staff all season long, helping to keep his team in contention until the final weeks.

The most unsung hero of the four might have had the best year: Andy Messersmith of the Dodgers. In 322 innings pitched—most in the NL—Andy hurled a league-leading 19 complete games, seven of them shutouts (also a high). He finished third in strikeouts. And despite being shut out five times and leaving the game tied in extra innings another five times, Messersmith posted 19 victories. With only an average amount of luck, he might well have enjoyed a 25-win season.

The writers picked Seaver, and they can't be faulted. But who would you have picked?

IN LATE JULY, 1975, the Milwaukee Brewers were mired in a slump that would eventually lead to an abysmal won-lost record of 68-94. At the same time, center-fielder Gorman Thomas was on his way to notching a season's batting average of .179. Poor Thomas had struck out in his last ten at-bats—one short of the record for a non-pitcher.

As Thomas stepped to the plate, the Milwaukee fans tensed in anticipation of the woeful feat they were about to witness. The pitch came in. Thomas connected! Unfortunately, he hit into a double play.

No matter—when the dejected young slugger trudged out to center field in the bottom of the inning, the relieved fans awarded him a standing ovation.

OPENING DAY 1975 at Cleveland's Memorial Stadium marked the managerial debut of Frank Robinson—and coincidentally, baseball's first managerial debut by a black man. One of Robinson's shrewdest strategical maneuvers this day occurred before the first pitch, when he penciled in his own name as the designated hitter. His next stroke of genius occurred in the first inning, when manager Robinson instructed player Robinson to hit a home run, which he did.

Eight more innings of Robby's leadership resulted in a 5-3 win over the Yankees, delighting over 56,000 Indian fans.

WHEN BASE-STEALING SPECIALIST Herb Washington was released by the Oakland A's early in the 1975 season, he left behind him one of the most puzzling statistical entries in the baseball record books: 31 stolen bases and not a single appearance at the plate.

The Greatest Series Ever?

As the 1975 World Series opened on a gray Saturday at Boston's Fenway Park, the question in the minds of most observers was not who would win the Series, but would the Red Sox provide any opposition to the juggernaut from Cincinnati?

Three hours later, the Sox had answered that question. Behind Luis Tiant, Boston dismantled the Big Red Machine by a score of 6-0. El Tiante, the ageless Cuban hurler with the pot belly and the shiny dome, set down the Reds on only five hits. And what is more, Looie started the big six-run rally with a single, his first hit in more than three years.

Game 2 presented much the same scenario: startlingly effective pitching by the Sox or sickly hitting by the Reds—depending on where one's rooting interest lay. Through eight innings, lefty Bill Lee held the Reds to four hits and a lone tally, while the Sox had picked up two runs. Even when Johnny Bench opened the ninth with a double to right, Sox fans were not overly concerned: Lee was replaced by relief specialist Dick Drago, who had been nothing short of sensational in the playoff series against Oakland. And sure enough, Drago retired Tony Perez on a bouncer and George Foster on a short fly to left. Only one out away from a two-game lead!

But at last, the Reds snapped out of their slumber and displayed the kind of battle-from-behind heroics that had brought them to the Series. A single by Dave Concepcion tied the game, and a long double by Ken Griffey drove in Concepcion. The Reds had been impressive in but one of eighteen innings in Boston, yet they were headed home for Riverfront Stadium in good shape.

Game 3 also opened up with little scoring, excellent defense, and fine pitching. But then the Reds exploded against Rick Wise to score two runs in the fourth and three more in the fifth. Those five runs seemed sufficient, even when a pinch-homer by ex-Red Bernie Carbo whittled the lead to 5-3. But the Red Sox were bent on revenge for the last-inning loss in Game 2. In the ninth, Dwight Evans reached reliever Rawly Eastwick for a two-run homer to knot the score.

In the bottom of the tenth, Cesar Geronimo opened with a single to right. Manager Sparky Anderson sent up seldom-used Ed Armbrister to bat for Eastwick. Armbrister's mission was obvious to everyone in the park: sacrifice. When he laid down a poor bunt right in front of the plate, catcher Carlton Fisk saw the opportunity to nail Geronimo at second. But as Fisk shed his mask and jumped out after the ball, Armbrister stepped out of the batter's box on his way to first base. The two collided. Fisk's hurried throw to second sailed into center field, and the Reds found themselves with a runner on third with no one out. Fisk protested heatedly that Armbrister should have been ruled out for interference. But umpire Larry Barnett let the play stand. Joe Morgan's single brought in Geronimo, and the Reds took a one-game lead in the Series.

Winning Game 4 was now a necessity for the Sox if they were to take the Series. Once again, their ace Tiant came through, struggling through 163 pitches to hang on to a 5-4 victory.

Game 5 was a laugher for the Reds. Tony Perez snapped out of an 0-for-15 slump with two gigantic home runs, and Don Gullett avenged his first-game loss. Completely overpowering, the young lefty allowed only two hits through the first eight innings before tiring in the ninth. The Reds now needed to win but one of the two games at Fenway.

Game 6 opened in fine style for Boston fans as rookie hero Fred Lynn walloped a three-run homer. With Luis Tiant again on the mound, a seventh game seemed assured. But after being baffled for four innings, the Reds reached Tiant for a couple of big hits in the fifth to tie the score at 3. George Foster's double in the seventh drove in two more runs. And when Cesar Geronimo tagged Tiant for a solo homer in the top of the eighth, Fenway Park settled into a deep gloom. The stellar Cincinnati bullpen had held the Sox in check since Lynn's opening-inning blast; the firemen seemed invincible.

With Pedro Borbon on the mound, Lynn led off the bottom of the eighth with a ground single. The next batter, Rico Petrocelli, walked. The fans at Fenway revived—their Sox still had a shot! Dwight Evans stepped to the plate as the potential tying run. But Rawly Eastwick replaced Borbon, and set Evans down on strikes. Then he retired Rick Burleson on a popup. That left the matter up to Bernie Carbo, hitting for reliever Rogelio Moret. Carbo had poled out a pinch-homer in the third game. Could he do it again? Yes, he could!

In the ninth, the Sox loaded the bases with no one out. The winning run seemed certain. But now it was the Reds's turn for heroics, as George Foster threw Denny Doyle out at the plate as Doyle attempted to score on Lynn's fly ball.

In the bottom of the eleventh, with Griffey on first base and one out, Joe Morgan lined a ball to deep right, headed for the stands. But Dwight Evans ran back, leaped, and somehow made the catch. Then he whirled and threw to first base to double up Griffey—who, like everyone else, had thought the ball a sure extra-base hit.

Later, Evans himself said, "I didn't think I had a chance."

Pete Rose said of Evans: "If he makes catches like that all the time, I don't ever want to hit one to right. . . . It was like he had magnets in his glove."

Inspired by this reprieve, the Sox wasted no time putting the game away. The first man up in the twelfth, Carlton Fisk, hit a long homer off the foul pole in left field to win the game, 7-6.

Though Game 7 was another thriller, it could not seem anything but anticlimactic to Game 6, which many observers were calling the most exciting Series game ever played. The Red Sox jumped off to a 3-0 lead and southpaw Bill Lee mystified the Reds with his mixture of junk deliveries and occasional hard stuff. But in the sixth inning, Lee tried to slip a "blooper" by Tony Perez, who had been fooled by the pitch on several other trips. Lee went to the well once too often. Perez waited on the ball and sent it rocketing off into the horizon beyond the left-field wall. A single by Pete Rose in the next inning knotted the score at 3. Once more, the Reds' bullpen had held the fort while the batsmen warmed to their task.

In the ninth, the Reds finally went ahead on a bloop single by Joe Morgan. The Red Sox went down in order in their half of the inning, and the 1975 World Series was history.

The Red Sox gave Cincinnati a contest, all right. Not only did they keep the issue in doubt until the final inning of the final game, but they missed a victorious four-game sweep by the slimmest of margins.